Disruptive Innovation in Indian Telecom Sector

A Case Study of Reliance Jio Infocomm Limited

DR. AYUSH KUMAR

Copyright © Dr. Ayush Kumar 2025
All Rights Reserved.

ISBN

Hardcase 979-8-89906-842-3
Paperback 979-8-89906-288-9

CONTENTS

PREFACE

In recent years, the Indian telecommunications sector has undergone a dramatic transformation—one that has not only redefined market dynamics but also reshaped the way millions of Indians connect, communicate, and consume information. At the center of this revolution stands Reliance Jio Infocomm Limited, whose entry into the market triggered an unprecedented wave of disruption. This book aims to explore the strategic underpinnings of Jio's rise through the lens of disruptive innovation.

The idea for this work emerged from a deep interest in understanding how disruptive forces take shape in emerging markets, particularly in industries that are traditionally seen as rigid and dominated by legacy players. The Indian telecom sector, with its complex regulatory landscape, massive customer base, and fierce competition, provided the perfect ground for such an inquiry.

Drawing upon Clayton Christensen's theory of disruptive innovation, this book presents a detailed case study of how Jio not only entered a mature industry but fundamentally altered its trajectory. Through strategic use of technology, aggressive pricing, and an integrated digital ecosystem, Jio not only captured market share but also set new benchmarks for service delivery, accessibility, and affordability.

The objective of this book is twofold. First, it seeks to provide a comprehensive academic analysis of Jio's strategy using established theoretical frameworks. Second, it aims to serve as a practical reference for students, business professionals, and policymakers who wish to understand how innovation can act as a powerful catalyst for change in high-stakes industries.

I am deeply grateful to the researchers, industry experts, and scholars whose work and insights have informed this study. I also acknowledge the millions of consumers whose responses to Jio's offerings helped shape the course of this disruption. This book is a tribute to the transformative power of innovation—and a reminder that even the most established industries can be reimagined.

– [Dr. Ayush Kumar]

01

INTRODUCTION

"Even the most successful organisations can find things they can improve on, and indeed, to avoid the innovator's dilemma, it's vital that successful businesses continue looking for ways they can improve."

– Clayton Christensen

This chapter begins with delineation on the significance of undertaking a research on Disruptive Innovation Strategy in Indian Telecom Sector with reference to Jio Infocomm Ltd. Thereafter, the objectives of the study, scope of the study and the organization of the book have been spelled out.

GENESIS

The Latin word "innovare," that means "to renew," is where the word "innovation" comes from. In essence, the word still means the same thing as it did when it was first used. To innovate is to make something better or change it. This could be a method, a product, or a service. But the phrase needs more explanation when it comes to business. In the business world, which is very complicated, you need a definition.

DEFINING INNOVATION

Innovation is putting ideas into action in a way that makes new products or services available or makes the ones that are already available better.

ISO TC 279 says that innovation is "a new or changed entity that creates or redistributes value" in the standard ISO 56000:2020. Others have different ideas about what innovation is, but all of them focus on the new, the better, and the dissemination of ideas or technologies.

Innovation often happens when people come up with better products, services, technologies, works of art, or business models and make them available to markets, governments, and society as a whole. Innovation is related to invention, but it is not the same thing. Innovation is more likely to involve using an invention (a new or better way of doing something) in the real world to make a big difference in a market or society. However, not all innovations necessitate a fresh invention. When a technical or scientific problem needs to be solved, technical innovation often comes about through the engineering process.

> Innovation is a key part of entrepreneurship, whether it's in an established business, a public service organisation, or a new business started by one person in the kitchen. It is how the entrepreneur creates new resources that can be used to make money or gives existing resources more potential to make money.
>
> *– Peter Drucker*

The steps needed to come up with new ideas, processes, or products that, when put into action, bring about positive, effective change. While invention is the process of coming up with new ideas, processes, or products, innovation is the process of putting those ideas into action. Innovation also involves a set of values that tries to get something good out of the act of coming up with something new. For example, actions that lead to a negative performance metric wouldn't be considered innovative, although if they met the requirements for being new and enabling actions.

– Marc Chason, Motorola Labs

Innovation is making something new that has value or finding a new way to get value. The key word is "value," which shows how innovation is different from invention. The definition is simple, memorable, and covers innovation in all parts of the value chain.

– Victor Fernandes, Natura

Innovation is just something new that your business does to meet a customer need that hasn't been met yet. The innovation should make a new market.

– Jonathan Rowe, Gene Express Inc

An innovation is a new idea that can be used in the real world. For a company, this is a process, product, business idea, or a combination of these things that has been put to use in the market and is bringing in new money and helping the company grow. I make a distinction between radical & disruptive innovation and incremental innovation, because incremental innovation can happen if a company is good at what it already does. True innovation is much more than just adding on to what's already being done, and while it's different, it uses skills that a company already has or that are added to by strategic partnerships. So, something is innovative not just because it's new to that business, but because it's new in general.

– Dr. Makarand "Chips" Chipalkatti, Osram Slyvania

Innovation is a way for a company to get new ideas, new ways to do things, or new products. In the past, innovation in the United States has been restricted to looking for a *"big"* idea to make a company more competitive. Management seems to be looking for a *"silver bullet"* or a new *"iPhone"* all the time, but real innovation is when every employee looks around his\her work area to find small problems and is given the power and responsibility to solve them. The average Japanese company gets 24 ideas from each employee every year and saves $4,000 per worker as a result. When all employees work together on continuous improvement, quality and productivity will get better every day, and great business ideas will "pop" out of nowhere.

– Norman Bodek, PCS Inc.

IMPORTANCE OF INNOVATION

1. **Solving Problems:** If the business offers services, it may realise that its customers don't have a way to tell it what they think, what they don't like, or what they like about the business. So, to address the problem, you might choose to run a virtual office in which customers' needs can be met quickly. Customers will be happy, and your sales will go up because of that.

2. **Adapting to Change:** Change is inevitable, and innovation is the way to not only keep your business going, but also make sure it stays relevant and profitable. So, if you build a culture of innovation, you will always be relevant.

3. **Maximizing on Globalization:** The markets across the world are becoming more connected, and in these new markets, more opportunities are opening up. For example, if your company wants to get a piece of this market share, it needs to come up with new ideas so it can take advantage of the new opportunities.

4. **Competing with Others:** If you want your company to stay ahead of the pack or get there in the first place, you need a dynamic business that can make smart, creative moves that set it apart from the rest.

5. **Evolving Workplace Dynamics:** The types of people who work there are always changing. So, innovation is important to make sure the company runs smoothly. Changes in customers' tastes and preferences: The current customer can choose from a wide range of products and services. So, the company needs to keep up with how customer tastes change and find new ways to meet their needs.

PROCESS OF INNOVATION

Step 1: Idea Generation and Mobilization –

During idea generation, new ideas are made. To come up with good ideas, one should feel a sense of competition and freedom to explore. When an idea is shifted to a new logical or physical place, this is called "mobilisation." For example, Apple waited 3 years after the MP3 players came out before making the iPod, which looked good, was easy to use, and could hold up to 1,000 songs.

Step 2: Advocacy and Screening –

It helps to figure out if a business idea is possible and what problems and benefits it might have. So, a choice can be made about what will happen to an idea. If a company wants to build a culture, it can set up a few best practises. For example, there should be many ways for employees to get help and feedback. Also, organisations need to understand how hard it is to judge ideas that are truly new. Also, organisations need to make evaluation and screening procedures that are clear.

Step 3: Experimentation –

During the experimentation stage, ideas are put to the test to see if they can work for an organisation at a certain time. Experiments help people come up with new ideas by giving them information about how well the original idea worked and whether or not it was possible. When Amazon tried out its delivery of groceries in some Seattle suburbs, for example. After that, Amazon Fresh went to San Diego, Los Angeles, and New York.

Step 4: Commercialization –

By focusing on how an idea affects people, commercialization makes it more valuable on the market. Putting together the details of an idea is an important step. At the commercialization stage, the focus shifts from development ident to persuasion. After the idea has been figured out and a business plan has been made, it will be ready to be shared and used.

Step 5: Spread the word and put it into action –

Diffusion is when everyone in the company agrees with a new idea, and implementation is when everything is set up to make the idea work. The organisation can figure out the next set of customer needs through diffusion and implementation. The organisation can speed up the innovation process by receiving feedback, indicators for success metrics, as well as other benchmarks.

TYPES AND EXAMPLES OF INNOVATION

- **Product Innovation:** Product innovation is the creation of a new product, like the Fitbit or the Kindle from Amazon, or an improvement to an existing product, like making the iPhone's digital camera resolution better. It could also be a new part of a product that already exists, like power windows on a car.

  Here are some examples of new products: The first electric cars that came out on the market were also an example of innovation, as are the new batteries that keep coming out with longer ranges.

- **Service Innovation:** Food delivery is a clear example of a new way to offer a service. For a long time, people who wanted to eat at a restaurant had to go there in person or call for takeout. That's when the market came up with a new idea: delivery service, so customers could call and order anything they wanted. Over time, it's become possible to buy food through websites. Now, we can buy food through mobile apps.

- **Process Innovation:** The process uses a mix of skill sets, facilities, and technologies to make, support, & deliver a product or service.

  Examples of Process innovations: The Henry Ford's invention was the world's first assembly line for cars. This process changed how cars are put together, cutting the time it takes to make one car from 24 hrs to 90 minutes. For, Grupo Bimbo's the Differential company developed a mobile sales dashboard. With a mobile sales dashboard, the team can quickly see sales data and other key performance indicators (KPIs) for each country.

- **Business Model Innovation:** In a business model innovation, the goal of transformation will be to improve a company's skills or processes so that it can be successful and make money.

  Business Model innovations Examples: Amazon's use of technology to find a new way to sell by cutting out the traditional retail channel and building direct relationships with customers. IBM has kept up with the changes in what it offers customers, from mainframes to PCs to technology services.

- **Organizational Innovation:** It is the process of coming up with a new strategy for an organisation. This means making changes to how the company does business, how work is organised, and how it works with outside stakeholders.

  Organizational innovations Examples: the fact that the companies switched to a four-day work week. The companies that began to use the digital power and let their workers work from home were the most successful.

- **Logistical Innovation:** A letter could take up to one month to arrive by mail for a long time. On average, it would take three months for goods from other countries. To fix this, businesses and distributors got creative with logistics by making storage points & strategic distribution centres. There are apps that let you hire courier services and even drones that can make deliveries.

- **Marketing innovation:** It means coming up with a new way to market that brings about change. For example, designing, packing, and making other decisions about a product's price or how to market it.

Example of innovative marketing: Touch Packaging Design and Nestlé Ice Cream have worked together to make a durable, reusable container for Haagen-Dazs that can be utilized in the new Loop circular online marketplace.

RISKS OF THE INNOVATION PROCESS AND THEIR SOLUTIONS

- **Technological Failure of the Innovation:** When a company comes up with a new product or idea, the biggest risk is whether or not it will work once it is released. To deal with this threat, the company may do small-scale tests to see how well it works. So, once this is done, the changes that need to be made can be made so that huge losses don't happen when the product is made in large quantities.
- **Financial Strain:** The process of coming up with new ideas can use up a lot of the company's money. This is because the returns are usually over a long period of time instead of right away. So, if this is done, the necessary changes can be made to avoid big losses when the product is made in large quantities.
- **Market Failure:** If a new product or technology doesn't do well when it's put on the market, it means that demand is low and the innovation isn't good for business. So, you should do a lot of research on the market before putting your limited resources into developing and making it.
- **Redundancy:** Because of the way the market moves, an innovation that is profitable today may not be in a few years. To stay one step ahead, there should be constant research into how to improve the systems that are already in place and what affects them.
- **Lack of Capacity for Implementation:** It's always risky to not have the structure and money to put the new idea into action. You could search for partners who really can help you in your weak spot and help you get over the problem.

- **Organizational Risks**: These risks have to do with how the business is set up and run. So, making sure you plan and use your resources well can help make sure this doesn't happen.
- **Unprecedented Risks:** These could be things like policy shifts or political instability that have a ripple effect that makes the innovation less useful. So, the business needs to have a plan for what to do in case something unexpected happens.

THE INNOVATION MATRIX

One of the most common ways of looking at innovation is via the Innovation Matrix, which is included below.

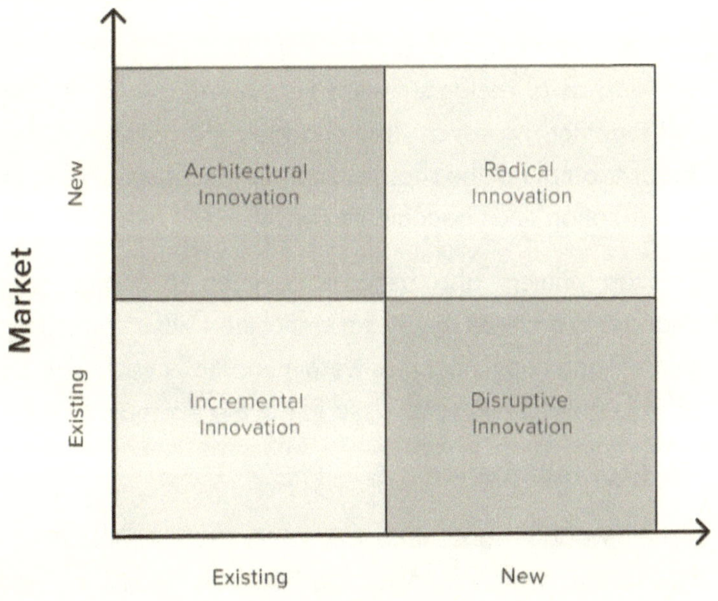

Figure 1.1

The Innovation Matrix classifies innovations according to both the technology it uses and the market it operates in. Therefore, it allows us to conceive of four distinct forms of innovation:

- ## Architectural Innovation

  Architectural innovation, which is also called "recombinant" innovation, is when a method, technology, or approach from one field is used in another. With architectural innovation, we take a product or service that already exists, break it down, & rebuild it for the new consumers. Architectural innovation is changing solutions that already work for a whole new market. Changing the total design of a product by placing its parts together in new ways is called architectural innovation. This change will happen in the next few days to a few years.

  Examples of architectural innovation

  Think about the app Uber. Sharing rides, using geolocation, and working as a freelancer were not new ideas. When they were put together, however, they changed the game and became a great example of the sharing economy, so much so that the word "uberization" has become its own word.

  Desktop printers also became common in homes because of changes in architecture. By the end of the 1980s, large commercial printers and copy machines were in most offices. The typical home office, on the other hand, used to have a dot matrix printer.

- ## Radical Innovation

  When we talk about innovation, we usually talk about radical innovation, which involves starting new industries and using "revolutionary" technologies. Radical innovations need radical thinking, and they are often linked to scientific and technological breakthroughs. So, even though it's a rare form of innovation, it's been credited with helping society make big steps forward.

  Examples of radical innovation

  From the Awakening and the Renaissance to the Industrial Revolution, history is full of examples of big changes. All of these times made people think deeply about how they live and how they relate to the world around them. Many people say that we are on the verge of the Fourth Industrial Revolution. They think that AI, 3D printing, and the Internet of Things (IoT) will induce big changes in fields ranging from transportation to healthcare.

Smartphones are a great example of a revolutionary new idea. What's interesting about smartphones is that they made us stop being so focused on making things smaller and made us rethink what a handheld device could do. No matter if we use our phones to talk, travel, or shop online, we can't deny how important they are to our daily lives. This is a sign of radical innovation.

- **Incremental Innovation**

The vast majority of innovations are small steps forward. Incremental innovation, also called "sustaining innovation," is the process of making small changes to products or services that are already on the market to make them more valuable to customers. It focuses on reducing errors and improving performance in small steps by adding features like expanding product lines, lowering costs, and making next-generation products.

Examples of incremental innovation

Some of the most well-known companies in the world have stayed at the top because they keep making small improvements. Even if you don't notice, many "legacy" brands are becoming industry mainstays because they don't let themselves get comfortable. As an example, let's look at Gillette. Since they made the first "safety" razor, they have made small changes to their product to make it better fit customer needs.

Amazon is a good example of a company that makes small changes over time. Amazon is such a huge company around the world that calling it a "global juggernaut" is a huge understatement. They got to this point by steadily improving their services. This includes adding next-day delivery and always trying new things with their website, which makes the user experience better every day.

- **Disruptive Innovation**

  The late Clayton Christensen popularised the term "Disruptive Innovation," is innovation that creates a new market and value network or enters at the bottom of an existing market and eventually displaces established market-leading firms, products, and alliances. When new products and technologies are made to fulfill a need in an existing market, this is called disruptive innovation. This kind of innovation is made possible by new technology that makes what's already on the market more efficient and easier to use. Businesses use disruptive innovation to meet the changing needs of their customers by making completely new value streams and service offerings that didn't exist before.

  Christensen's theory says that new products usually enter the marketplace at a lower performance point, at least when measured by the traditional measures of that market. Still, they provide value in a different way to a part of the market where that feature is very important. Then, this small piece of the market is used to quickly grow and shake up the whole market.

  People probably use disruptive innovations like Netflix and the grocery store chain Aldi on a regular basis. In the end, risk-takers rise to the top in a competitive market, and these two companies are great examples of how disruptive innovation should be done.

DEFINING DISRUPTIVE INNOVATION

"Disruptive innovation refers to the innovation that transforms expensive or highly sophisticated products or services—previously accessible to a high-end or more-skilled segment of consumers—to those that are more affordable and accessible to a broader population. This transformation disrupts the market by displacing long-standing, established competitors."

"Disruptive innovation is the process by which a smaller company usually with fewer resources moves upmarket and challenges larger, established businesses."

The process begins with a small company entering the low end of a market, or creating a new market segment, claiming the least profitable portion of the market as its own. Because the established, incumbent companies own the most profitable market segments, they most likely won't fight the entrant for that market share.

Disruptive innovation is not the process of improving or enhancing products for the same target group; rather, it involves the technologies used to make them easy to use and available to the larger, non-targeted market. An example of disruptive innovation is the introduction of digital music downloads, which have, by far, replaced compact discs (CDs).

Clayton Christensen pioneered the concept of disruptive innovation in his book 'The Innovator's Solution', the follow-up to his 1997 book 'The Innovator's Dilemma'. Christensen hypothesised that businesses engage with two kinds of technology. Sustainable technologies are ones that allow a company to progressively enhance its operations over a certain period of time. These technologies and the manner in which they were implemented in the company were created largely to enable corporations to stay competitive, or at the very least, to maintain the status quo. The disruptive technologies and the manner in which they were incorporated—the disruptive innovations—were more difficult to plan for and possibly more damaging to businesses that did not give them adequate consideration.

Investing in a disruptive innovation is difficult. Rather than focusing on the advancement of the technology itself, an investor must consider how firms will react to disruptive technologies. Google (GOOGL), Amazon

(AMZN) and Meta (FB) previously Facebook, are examples of corporations that have placed a significant emphasis on the internet as a disruptive technology. Companies that failed to incorporate disruptive innovation into their strategic planning have been pushed aside since the internet has become so pervasive in the modern world. Artificial intelligence and its capacity to learn from people and execute their tasks may soon be a game-changing breakthrough for the whole labour market.

What constitutes a technology or invention "disruptive" is debatable. This word may be applied to technologies that are not genuinely disruptive. The Internet was disruptive since it was not an evolution of prior technologies. It was something novel that generated never-before-seen models for producing money. Other business strategies clearly suffered as a result of this.

People utilising smartphones rather than laptops and desktops for personal computing requirements, such as online surfing & streaming, is another illustration of disruptive innovation. These functions are supported by miniature processors, chips, and software programmes that have been made possible by technological advances. Smartphone developers addressed the vast market of mobile customers with cellular devices that find it cumbersome to carry and use computers when surfing the web. Smartphones are compact, readily portable and storable, and relatively inexpensive compared to desktops and laptops.

In contrast, the Model T car is not seen as a typical example of disruptive innovation due to the fact that it was an upgrade on an existing technology that was not widely embraced upon its debut. The automobile industry did not take off until mass manufacturing lowered costs and shifted the whole transportation system from horses to wheels. In this regard, the mass-production system meets the requirements for disruptive innovation.

Example of Amazon

The way the bookselling business was changed by the internet is a perfect illustration of how the internet's innovations can be disruptive. Amazon

(AMZN) beat out the big bookselling chains because it could show its stock without having to have a store in every town and ship the book to the customer's house. Before online purchasing became very popular, people bought books in conventional bookshops.

Amazon's profits as well as market share grew in line with its popularity, putting many bookstores out of business or on the back shelf. Since its start, Amazon has been able to utilise the internet to establish a platform for online shopping. Most of what you can buy in a store, including groceries, can be purchased from Amazon's website. And it all started with a small company that started in a garage and used the potential of the internet to meet the needs of an online shopping niche market.

Example of Netflix

Netflix is another company that is shaking things up. At a time when there were a lot of video stores where you could rent VHS tapes and DVDs, Netflix saw an opportunity to serve an untapped market of online customers. Using the rising potential of the internet, they gave customers the chance to look through their library of DVDs, rent what they wanted without worrying about someone else renting the same thing, and have their choices sent straight to their homes.

Not long after they started renting DVDs by mail, they changed their business model and found a way to shake up the market by streaming entertainment online. But now, Netflix's competitors have been able to successfully copy this business model, which hurts Netflix's market share. It's time and the market that will show how long Netflix can stay on top, but there's no question that they caused a big disruption in the market. After Netflix changed the media business, Blockbuster reduced its number from more than 9,000 stores to just one, which is now known as Airbnb.

HISTORICAL PERSPECTIVE OF DISRUPTIVE INNOVATION

Clayton M. Christensen came up with the term "disruptive technology." He used it for the first time in an article he wrote with Joseph Bower in

1995 called "Disruptive Technologies: Catching the Wave." The article is written for both business managers who decide how much money to spend or what to buy and researchers, who are largely responsible for bringing the disruptive vector to the retail market. In his book "The Innovator's Dilemma," he says more about the term. In the 1990s, Christensen was told that the disc drive and memory industry were to the study of technology what fruit flies were to the study of genetics. In Innovator's Dilemma, Christensen looked at the cases of the disc drive industry and the excavating as well as earth-moving industries (where hydraulic actuation slowly, yet eventually, displaced cable-actuated machinery). In his follow-up book, The Innovator's Solution, which he wrote with Michael E. Raynor, Christensen changed the term "disruptive technology" to "disruptive innovation." He did this because he realised that most technologies are not inherently disruptive or sustaining. Instead, it is the business strategy that identifies the key idea that leads to huge market success and then acts as the "disruptive vector." But understanding Christensen's business model, that shows how the disruptive vector goes from an idea in the mind of the innovator to a product that can be sold, is key to understanding how new technology makes it easier for the disruptor to quickly destroy established technologies and markets. Christensen and Mark W. Johnson, who started the management consultancy firm Innosight with each other, wrote an article called "Reinventing Your Business Model" for the Harvard Business Review in 2008. In it, they explained how "business model innovation" works. The idea of disruptive technology is a continuation of a long-standing practise of economists who study innovation and the people in charge of putting new ideas into action at an enterprise or policy level.

Christensen says that the term "disruptive innovation" is misleading if it is used to describe the "instantaneous value" of a product or service's market behaviour instead of its "integral" or "sum over history" behaviour.

In the late 1990s, the automotive industry started to work with consultant David E.O'Ryan to adopt the idea of "constructive disruptive technology." This meant combining current off-the-shelf technology with newer innovations to create what O'Ryan called "an unfair advantage." The process or technological change as a whole had to be "constructive" in enhancing the current way of making things, but it also had to have a disruptive effect on the whole business case model and lead to a big drop in waste, energy, materials, labour, or legacy costs for the user.

Christensen's theory describes why many disruptive innovations really aren't advanced or useful technologies, which is what a default hypothesis would lead one to think. This is in line with the idea that a convincing advertising campaign may be just as effective at bringing a successful and effective product to market as advanced technology. Rather, they are often clever combinations of off-the-shelf components that are applied to a small value network that is just starting out.

TechRepublic, an online news site, says that the term and similar terms should not be used anymore because, as of 2014, they are overused jargon.

Its strategy has partly worked, as can be seen by the fact that it has gained close to 200 million new subscribers. But it's still not clear if these customers will stick with it once the initial excitement caused by freebies and subsidies wears off and the subsidies end.

NATURE AND CHARACTERISTICS OF DISRUPTIVE INNOVATION

Clayton Christensen, a professor at Harvard Business School and expert on disruption, says that a disruption "replaces an existing market, industry, and technology with something new, better, and more valuable." It's both bad and good at the same time."

In today's business world, which is very competitive and full of change, many large companies are being replaced by smaller ones that are growing quickly. This is clear because the average length of time a company was in the S&P 500 was 33 years in 1964, but it was only 24 years in 2016, and it is expected to be only 12 years by 2027. So, today's leaders not only have to make sure that their own organisations keep getting results and making money, but they also have to plan for the future by figuring out how to beat the disruptive forces that will be working against them in the future. Leaders should first understand such five things about disruption in order to do this.

- **Disruption is FAST:** The pace of disruption is due to how quickly technology is changing, which has led to shortened business cycles and fast growth. Because of this, the rate of change has sped up much more quickly. Xiaomi and Slack, for example, were valued at $1 billion in less than two years. It took the TV 13 years to achieve 50 million users, while Facebook did take 3.5 years and Pokemon Go only 19 days. The fact that "disruption is always on" also means that organisations can't rest on their laurels or think they have a lot of time to respond to disruptions.

- **Disruption is UNPREDICTABLE:** The influence of disruption are spreading from one industry to another. No one is protected from disruption, and it doesn't have to be a traditional competitor trying to get a piece of the same market. It could also be a relatively unknown competitor from the outside. For example, Hilton Worldwide as well as InterContinental Hotels Group might be your main competitors if you're Marriott, the largest hotel chain in the world based on market capitalization. You won't expect a company that doesn't own any properties to try to take your share of the market. Airbnb is now the largest provider of places to stay in the world. This means that one of the main advantages of disruptors is that they can catch organisations by surprise, so organisations must always be ready and on guard.

- **Disruption is PERMISSIONLESS:** It don't follow the laws, rules, or regulations that are already in place. They can play by new regulations by coming up with clever ways to get around any policy or rule set by regulators. This means that incumbents can't always rely on rules and regulators to safeguard their model or market share, because disruptors can often find a way to compete, grow, and take market share. When Uber came along and changed the taxi business, they said that ride-sharing is not the same as hailing a taxi, so taxi regulations don't apply to them. Before the government stepped in, Uber had grown quickly in much more than 100 cities from 2010 to 2014.

- **Disruption is MESSY:** It changes the way business is done and how people have been successful in the past. Organizations need to realise that "what got them here won't get them there" and make sure they have the power and skills to disrupt themselves before others do. People often use Kodak as an example because they made the first hand - held digital camera in 1975 but didn't sell it because it would cut into their very successful sales of film and cameras. They went bankrupt in 2012 because they didn't know how to deal with the widespread use of digital photography. Organizations tend to defend there extremely successful as well as proven business model, but they can't wait until something is broken to fix it, because disruption can create and extract value through business models that are both new and destructive. It's a messy process to change your own profitable and successful business model, product, or service.

- **Disruption is DEADLY:** The most important thing about disruption is that it can put businesses out of business. Many companies have gone out of business because they couldn't compete with their disruptors and had to file for bankruptcy. Blockbuster and Borders are just two examples of companies that failed to compete to disruptors like Netflix and Amazon because they didn't think they could. This is what led to their demise.

Most people agree that change is inevitable; it's just a question of when, not if. Leaders must know what disruption is and how they need to lead differently in order to be successful. One reason why it's hard for existing companies to take advantage of disruptive innovations is that the things that make them good at their current business—like their leadership style, processes, and business model—make them bad in competing to the disruption. And if leaders wait to put in time and effort until they know they have to, it's likely that it will be too late.

BENEFITS OF DISRUPTIVE INNOVATION

The process existed long before Clayton Christenson came up with this word. True entrepreneurs and leaders understand the effects and benefits of disruptive technology to the core, and they are aware of the following benefits.

- Helpful in growing the market with new ideas
- Creating a culture that embraces change instead of ignoring it.
- Revamping and updating the current set of traditional policies and practices.
- It's easy to spot people who are open to change and optimistic about technology.

In today's economy, disruptive technology is more than a new idea. It's a chance to go further than the current finish and get better. Businesses can avoid risks and stay in business in a competitive market if they are willing to accept breakdowns. Businesses all over the world need to make it a habit to invest in new ideas if they want to grow.

- **Technology Transfer**

  Technology is often moved from one sector to another through innovation, so that its full potential can be used in different fields and efficiency can be raised. For example, when a supermarket utilises solar energy to make electricity, it helps save the environment by cutting down on greenhouse gas emissions.

- **Be at the Forefront of the Market**

  If a business doesn't try new things, its competitors will pass it by. A business can go out of business if it doesn't keep up with the market. For example, if a bank doesn't offer online banking services, customers will look for other banks where they can use these services.

- **Increased Sales**

Innovative products do better than others because they get people's attention, which leads to sales. This helps the company make more money. For example, if a supermarket puts out new products, people who want to buy that products will come to the store, which will bring in more money for the company.

- **Improving Efficiency**

When a company innovates, it saves time and money that would otherwise be spent on things that aren't productive. For eg, when an office buys software that automatically perform administrative tasks, employees have a little more time to focus on growing the business and helping customers. Some of the benefits of utilizing a disruptive business model for your company are listed here.

- **Support to start-ups**

It is very hard for new businesses in the country to prove their worth and get a foothold among the conventional giants that are already there. The person who comes up with this kind of new idea would have a chance to expand quickly and do better than the companies that are already out there.

- **An opportunity for business growth**

Even though it gives new businesses a chance to get a stronger hold on the market, if existing businesses adopt disruptive innovation as part of their innovation culture, they can take advantage of even more great opportunities and grow their businesses.

- **Expansion of the market**

  The main benefit of putting this innovation culture into place in one's company is that it will help to grow the market more than one's usual methods. Innovations that are disruptive have made it possible for consumers to change how they act in traditional industries. At first, it may not seem to work, but after a while, you can see the real result.

IMPORTANCE OF DISRUPTIVE INNOVATION

Although innovation has always been considered an important element within the business world, today this term has become much more valuable. To me, it's now being seen more as a necessity than an option. Here's why, I believe disruption is important:

➢ **To the Industry or Business**

- **Ahead of the Competition:** Driving innovation in business gives one an edge over the competition because it gives consumers and society new possibilities that other businesses haven't been able to offer yet.

- **Constant Transformation:** The Disruptive innovation is a constant change factor in the industry it is a part of because it brings about good change. When disruptive processes, which are the focus of innovation, are put into place, they cause big changes within the organization.

- **The Core is Still There:** Disruption is a term that is always changing, and its main goal is to give people a high quality of life. In business, people are always the most important thing. In the same way, companies that begin disruptive transformation processes from ultimate innovation make new products that meet their needs for improvement and growth.

- **Promotes Efficiency:** Disruptive innovation is always seen as a way to make things more efficient. In other words, this idea is about a company doing things that set it apart from its competitors. This can be done by optimising all of the key processes or opening new business projects.

➢ **To the Society**

- Disruptive innovation can make society better by attempting to bring about new levels of productivity, efficiency, and convenience. For eg, the personal computer (PCs) and the internet have made it simpler and quicker than ever for people to get information and talk to each other. This has made us both more efficient and productive at work and in our personal lives. But disruptions can also be bad for people and industries that can't adapt to the changes. For example, the traditional photography business has been hurt by digital photography. This has caused people to lose their jobs and photo labs all over the country to close.
- Problems that the status quo couldn't solve are better solved by disruptive technologies. They have the potential to change the world by making people more efficient, productive, and comfortable. But they may also hurt people and businesses that can't give in to them.
- A disruptive technology replaces systems or habits by making them obsolete because it is clearly better. E-commerce, online news websites, ride-sharing apps, & GPS systems are all recent examples of disruptive technologies.
- It has changed the way people work, live, and do business in a big way and the economy will grow.

FACTORS INFLUENCING THE MIGRATION OF CUSTOMERS FROM OTHER TELECOM PROVIDERS TO RELIANCE JIO

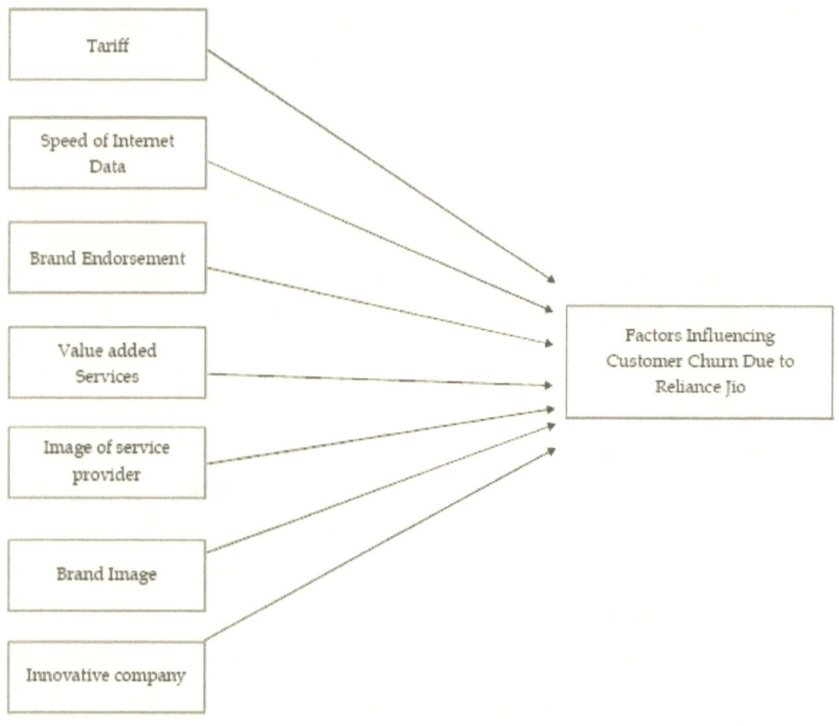

Figure 1.2

Source: *Jasrotia, S. S., Sharma, R. L., & Mishra, H. G. (2019) Disruptions in Indian Telecom Sector: A Qualitative Study on Reliance Jio.*

i. **Tariff/Fixed Price:** Indian customers care a lot about prices (Mahajan et.al, 2017). Price is one of the most important factors in developing & emerging markets like India's telecom sector market (Srivastava et.al. 2006). By offering free 4G data and voice calls, Reliance Jio has changed the Indian telecom market. It has gained a huge market share and has reached 100 million subscribers in just one year. Customers were very focused on price when they were being interviewed, and they said that Reliance Jio has the cheapest services in the country and has cut voice calling and data tariffs so much that their competitors are having a hard time keeping up. Because of this, many customers have switched from other operators to Reliance Jio.

ii. **Speed of Internet Data:** The number of people using the Internet is growing at a very fast rate, and users now care a lot about how fast they can connect (Kridel et.al, 2002). Customers want fast internet, but they have to pay more for it (Rappoport et.al, 2003). Reliance Jio started a new trend by making high-speed internet data cheaper and more accessible. Before Reliance Jio, telecom companies used to charge more for high-speed data. With the goal of being their clients' "first call," Reliance Jio is working very hard to reach that goal. Customers said they used to pay a lot for 2G and 3G internet services, but Reliance Jio has made 4G services cheaper than 2G services, which is a big deal in India.

iii. **Brand Endorsement:** An endorser and his or her message will make a customer like a product more, which will lead to positive feelings about that brand (Mowen, 1980). At first, Reliance used PM Modi in its ads, which influenced customers because he is a well-known public figure and the Prime Minister of India. This helped Reliance Jio support the success of the Digital India campaign and get more subscribers through word of mouth.

iv. **Value-added Services:** Value-added services (VAS) are popular in the telecom industry, but they are often offered at too high a price, which makes customers less likely to use them (Schultz, 2001). Users are very happy with the value-added services that Reliance Jio offers. They used to think that other telecom operators would charge extra money for any extra service or even take money off if they accidentally chose the wrong service, but Reliance Jio doesn't do that because they offer these services for free.

v. **Image of service provider:** The Image of service provider is a critically important factor that leads to customer satisfaction, and there is a positive association between image of service provider & customer satisfaction (Sandhu et.al, 2013). India's largest Corporate Social Responsibility (CSR) network is run by Mukesh Ambani, and Reliance industries gave Rs. 652 Crores to CSR activities in 2016. (India CSR, 2016). These things have given Reliance Industries a good name in the public eye, which makes it easier for them to get customers than its competitors.

vi. **Brand Image:** A company's brand image is a sign and a cause of customer satisfaction if it is good (Malik et.al, 2012). Another big reason why people use Reliance Jio is that it has built a strong brand image in just over a year and a half. Customers have started spreading the word about Reliance Jio, and it has such a good brand image that individuals have begun buying 4G phones they didn't have before just so they can use Reliance Jio's services.

vii. **Innovative Company:** Being innovative is one of the things that make up a service provider (Paulrajan and Rajkumar, 2011). Reliance Jio is a new, innovative company that is shaking up the telecom industry and pressuring other telecom companies to cut their prices so they can stay in business. Jio has come up with the notion of giving away for free services that other telecom companies used to charge a lot of money for.

RELIANCE JIO INFOCOMM LIMITED- PROFILE

Reliance Jio Infocomm Limited, doing business as Jio, is an Indian telecommunications company and a subsidiary of Jio Platforms. It has its main office in Navi Mumbai, Maharashtra, India. It runs an LTE network that covers the whole country and all 22 telecom circles. Jio has 4G and 4G+ service right now, but it is working on getting 5G and 6G service as well.

Jio had a soft launch on December 27, 2015, with a beta for partners and employees. On September 5, 2016, the public was able to use Jio. It has more than 42.62 crore (426.2 million) subscribers, making it the largest mobile network operator in the country and the third-largest in the world. In September 2019, Jio started a service called "fibre to the home." This service gives people Internet, TV, and phone services at home. As of Sept. 2020, Reliance Industries has raised 1.65 lakh cr. (US$21 billion) by selling nearly 33% of its equity stake in Jio Platforms.

On the eve of the 83rd birthday of the founder of Reliance Industries Late Dhirubhai Ambani, the services were first made available to Jio's employees and partners on December 27, 2015. The services were then made available to the public on September 5, 2016. Reliance Jio Infocomm Limited (RJIL), a subsidiary of Reliance Industries Limited (RIL), the country's largest private sector company, is the first telecom operator to hold a pan India Unified License. This licence lets RJIL offer all kinds of phone services except for the Global Mobile Personal Communication by Satellite Service.

RJIL owns spectrum in the 1800 MHz (in 14 circles) & 2300 MHz (in 22 circles), which means it can offer 4G wireless services. RJIL wants to offer 4G services that work well together using FDD-LTE on 1800 MHz & TDD-LTE on 2300 MHz as part of an integrated ecosystem.

RJIL is building a pan-India telecom network to serve the underserved India market with reliable high-speed internet (4th generation), rich communication services, and a wide range of digital services in key areas like education, health care, safety, financial services, government citizen interfaces, and entertainment. RJIL wants to give people access to new and useful digital content, apps, and services anytime and anywhere. This will help India become a world leader in the digital economy.

RJIL is also setting up an improved packet core network to build a high-capacity infrastructure for the future that can handle a lot of data and voice traffic. The 4G network will offer voice services from and to networks that are not part of the RJIL.

Reliance Jio is part of the "Bay of Bengal Gateway" Cable System, which is meant to connect South East Asia, South Asia, and the Middle East to Europe, Africa, and Far East Asia by connecting to other existing and recently built cable systems that land in India, the Middle East, and Far East Asia.

RJIL's subsidiary has been given a "FBO License" in Singapore, which lets it buy, operate, and sell undersea and/or terrestrial fibre connectivity, established its internet point of presence, offer internet transit as well as peering services, as well as data and voice roaming services in Singapore.

RJIL has finished key contracts with its technology partners, infrastructure providers, service providers, application partners, device manufacturers, as well as other strategic partners for the project. All such strategic partners have put in a lot of money, time, and knowledge to help with the planning, deployment, and testing that is going on right now.

Evolution of RJIL- History

Infotel Broadband Services Limited (IBSL) company was set up on February 15, 2007 in Ambawadi, Ahmedabad, Gujarat. In June 2010, Reliance Industries (RIL) paid 4,800 crore (about Rs.91 billion or US$1.1 billion) for a 95% stake in IBSL. Even though it wasn't publicly traded, IBSL was the only company to win broadband spectrum across all 22 circles in India during the 4G auction earlier that year. In January 2013, Infotel Broadband Services Limited changed its name to Reliance Jio Infocomm Limited (RJIL), but it still works as a telecom subsidiary of RIL.

Jio said in June 2015 that it would start doing business all over the nation by the end of 2015. But four months later, in October, the company put the launch off until the first quarter of the 2016–2017 financial year.

Later, in July 2015, an NGO named 'Centre for Public Interest Litigation', filed a PIL through Prashant Bhushan to challenge the Indian government's decision to give Jio a pan-India licence. The PIL also said that the company was allowed to offer voice telephony in addition to its

4G data service for an extra fee of just 165.8 crore (US$21 million). The PIL said that this was arbitrary and unreasonable, and that it cost the government 2,284.2 crore (US$290 million). The Indian Department of Telecommunications (DoT), on the other hand, said that the norms for 3G and Broadband Wireless Access (BWA) spectrum didn't stop BWA winners from offering voice telephony. So, the PIL was taken away, and the accusations were thrown out.

On December 27, 2015, the 4G services went live inside the company. The company started selling its 4G services on September 5, 2016, and they were free until December 31, 2016, but they were later extended until March 31, 2017. Jio announced that it had 16 million subscribers in the first month and 50 million subscribers 83 days after its launch. On February 22, 2017, it reached 100 million subscribers, becoming the first company to do so. By October 2017, about 130 million people had signed up for it.

MAJOR PRODUCTS AND SERVICES

1. **Mobile Broadband**

    In September 2016, the company brought its 4G broadband services to all of India. It was supposed to come out in December 2015, but some reports said the company was waiting for the government to give them the final permits. Jio has voice and data services that are based on the fourth-generation (4G) network. It also has services like instant messaging & streaming movies and music.

2. **Jio Fiber**

    In August 2018, Jio started testing a new fiber-to-the-home service called "Jio Giga Fiber." This service includes high-speed internet with speeds between 100 and 1000 Mbit/s, TV, and landline phone service. In August 2019, it was declared that the service would go live on September 5, 2019, under the name JioFiber. This was done to celebrate the third anniversary of the company. Jio also said that some JioFiber subscribers will be able to stream movies that are still in theatres. This will be called "First Day First Show." In 2015, the company had a network of more than 250,000 km (160,000 mi) of fibre optic cables across the country. It will work with local cable operators to connect more people to its broadband services through this network.

3. **Jio Business**

In March 2021, the company started offering connectivity solutions for businesses that came with services from Jio Platforms, Reliance Retail, and Office 365.

4. **Jio Branded Devices**

- **LYF smartphones:** In June 2015, Jio made a deal with the Indian phone maker Intex to provide voice over LTE-capable 4G phones (VoLTE). But in October 2015, Jio said that it would start selling its own brand of phones called LYF. On January 25, 2016, the company released its first smartphone in the LYF line, called Water 1, through its Reliance Retail chain of stores that sell electronics. So far, three more phone models have come out: Water 2, Earth 1, and Flame 1.

- **Jio Phone:** Jio also sold a line of simple phones called "feature phones." The first model came out in August 2017, and people could start pre-ordering it on August 24. It was marketed as an LTE-compatible feature phone that was "affordable." It runs on the KaiOS platform, which is based on the now-defunct Firefox OS. It has a 2.4-inch screen, a dual-core processor, 4 GB of storage, NFC, a package of Jio-branded apps (along with the voice assistant Hello Jio). It also works with a "TV cable" accessory that lets you send the output to a separate screen. In July 2018, the company showed off the JioPhone 2, an updated version with a QWERTY keyboard, a horizontal display, and a keyboard bar. Jio also said that the two phones would be able to use WhatsApp, Facebook and YouTube apps.

- **Jionet Wi-Fi:** Before its pan-India launch of 4G data and telephony services, the company began offering free Wi-Fi hotspots in cities all over India, such as Surat, Ahmedabad, and Visakhapatnam in Gujarat, Indore, Jabalpur, Dewas, and Ujjain in Madhya Pradesh, certain parts of Mumbai, Kolkata, Lucknow, Bhubaneswar, Mussoorie. In March 2016, Jio started giving away free Wi-Fi to people watching the 2016 ICC World Twenty20 matches at six cricket stadiums.

- **Jio Phone Next:** On June 24, 2021, Mukesh Ambani said that JioPhone Next would be coming out. It is a full-featured Android phone that was made in partnership with Google over a long period of time. On November 4, 2021, the cheap smartphone went on sale in India. The Pragati OS, which was made in India and is based on the Android Go OS, will run on the Jio Phone Next. This phone is an entry-level phone. It's meant to replace feature phones and do basic smartphone things well, but it doesn't have many features.

- **Jio-Fi Router:** Jio-Fi is a Wi-Fi internet router that you can take with you. It was made by Reliance. The 2G of the dongle has been on sale since the start of September. The JioFi WIFI router can attach to devices that aren't 4G. It can assist a large number more people due to this. The second-generation JioFi router costs Rs. 1999. The price for the new Jio-Fi is the same as it was for the old one. There are four versions of the JioFi Router, and they all look and have different specs.

- **JioFi 1 Router**: This was released as the first JioFi router.
- **JioFi 2 Router:** This version of JioFi 2 sells the most of all the versions that are still available at Jio stores.
- **JioFi 3 Router:** This is the improved version of JioFi 2 with new Oled on the front which shows you the battery strength, Network, and Connectivity.
- **JioFi 4 Dongle:** The JioFi dongle is the most recent addition to the JioFi series, but it's not yet in all stores. It may be used on a PC or laptop to connect to the Internet without any problems.

JioFi 2 Router Specifications

- Portable Wi-Fi hotspot connects to 10 devices and one on USB.
- Enjoy HD voice calls, video calls on 2G / 3G phone via Jio4GVoice app.
- The powerful 2300mAh battery which gives you a backup of 6 hours.
- JioFi Wi-Fi 33 router range easily cover 2 rooms.

- **Jio Apps**

In May 2016, Jio put a group of multimedia apps on Google Play as part of its plans to offer 4G services. Anyone can download the apps, but a Jio sim card is needed to use them. Most of the apps are also still in the "beta" stage. Here are all of the apps:

My Jio- Jio Account Management	**Jio Gate-** apartment security app
Jio TV- live TV streaming app	
Jio Cinema- video-on-demand app	**Jio Cloud-** cloud storage services
	Jio Security- security app
Jio Saavn- an online music streaming service	**Jio Health Hub-** health companion

Jio Chat- messaging app	**Jio POS Lite-** Jio recharge commission earning app
Jio Meet- video-conferencing platform	**Jio Gameslite-** Online gaming
Jio Store- app store for Jio STB	**Jio Money-** digital currency and payments services
Jio Pages- web browser	
Jio Pay- digital payments and financial services app	**Jio Mart-** online grocery delivery services (partnership with Reliance Retail)
Jio Switch- file sharing app	**Jio Sign-** online grocery delivery services (partnership with Reliance Retail)
Jio News- free newspaper and magazine app	
Jio Home- mobile remote control for Jio set-top box	

JIO PLANS AND OFFERS ANALYSIS

JIO's Offers at Introduction Level:

Launch of JIO into the market	Provide free SIM with registration of identity proof (only AADHAR) and mobile's bar code scanning of the user
Offers	Unlimited voice calls; free SMS, *unlimited data* and free roaming.
Validity of offers	5 months.

JIO's Offers at 2nd Level:

Availability of SIM in the market	Provide free SIM with registration of identity proof (only AADHAR).
Offers	Unlimited voice calls; free SMS, *4GB per day data* and free roaming.
Validity of offers	3 months.

JIO's Offers at 3rd Level:

Availability of SIM in the market	Provide free SIM with registration of identity proof (only AADHAR).
Offers	Unlimited voice calls; free SMS, 1GB per day data and free roaming.
Validity of offers	4 months

JIO's Offers at 4th Level: JIO Prime Membership

Existing Users	Users need to recharge Rs. 99 to get JIO Prime Membership to continue with already existing offers. Within a short period, they suddenly introduced *"JIO Dhan Dhana Dhan Offer"* where users need to recharge with Rs. 303 to continue their existing benefits for 3 month (90 Days)
New Users	A person who wants to buy a new Jio Sim first have to recharge with Rs. 99 to get Jio Prime membership and become a user of Jio. To get introduced *"Jio Dhan Dhana Dhan Offer"* new user recharge with Rs. 309 to get the service of Jio.

Table 1.1:

Source: *Salomi, I. S., & Selvan, G. (2017)*

Most Popular Current Plans of JIO (2022)

The most popular plan of Jio is Rs 666 with Unlimited Calling any Net, 1.5GB/day Data, 100 SMS/ Day for 84 Days and Rs. 719 with Unlimited Calling any Net 2GB/day Data, 100 SMS/ Day for 84 Days with all the bundle of free subscription of Jio Apps. Apart from the above Jio also launched Work from Home Data Pack during Lockdown period for the Working Class and Students for Online Classes.

RESEARCH METHODOLOGY

Research is "creative and systematic work undertaken to increase the stock of knowledge". It involves gathering, organising, and analysing information to learn more about a subject or problem. A research project might build on what has already been done in the field. To test how well instruments, processes, or experiments work, researchers may repeat parts of or the whole project. In its simplest form, research is the search for knowledge and the search for the truth. In a formal sense, it is a systematic study of a problem using a carefully chosen strategy. It starts with choosing an approach, making a plan (design), acting on it by making research hypothesis, choosing methods and techniques, and choosing or making tools for collecting data, analysing the data, figuring out what it all means, and presenting a solution or solutions to the problem. **John W. Creswell says**, "Research is a set of steps used to gather and analyse information to learn more about a topic or issue." It has three parts: asking a question, gathering information to answer the question, and giving an answer to the question. More specifically, the Merriam-Webster Online Dictionary defines research as "careful inquiry or examination; especially: investigation or experimentation designed to find and explain facts, change accepted theories or laws in light of new facts, or put these new or changed theories or laws to use in the real world."

Methodology "Methodology is the philosophical framework or foundation on which research is done" (Brown, 2006). O'Leary (2004) says that methodology is the framework for our research. This framework is based on a certain set of paradigmatic assumptions. Allan and Randy (2005) say that a research method must meet the following two requirements: **First**, the research method should be the best way to reach the goals of the study. **Second,** the same research methods should be able to be used in other studies of the same kind.

Research methodology is a way for a researcher to explain how they plan to do their research. It's a plan to fix a research problem that makes sense and is well thought out. A researcher's methodology describes how they will do their research to get reliable, valid outcomes that meet their goals and aims. It includes what data they're going to gather, where they're going to get it, and how they're going to get it and look at it. A research method gives research credibility and makes sure that the results are scientifically sound. It also gives researchers a detailed plan that assists them stay on track and makes the process easy to handle. The approach and methodologies used to come to a conclusion are explained in a researcher's methodology.

OBJECTIVES OF THE STUDY

1. To explore the concept of disruptive innovation in context of Indian telecom industry.

2. To examine the disruptive innovation Strategy adopted by the Reliance Jio Infocomm Limited.

3. To evaluate the factors of disruption in Indian telecom industry w.r.t. market players & consumers.

4. To study the impact of disruption on competitors of Reliance Jio Infocomm Limited.

5. To identify the change in values & benefits offered by telecom companies after disruptive innovation in Indian telecom industry.

SCOPE OF THE STUDY

1. The scope of the study was totally restricted up to Indian Telecom Industry and specially with reference to Reliance Jio Infocomm Limited.

2. When & where required other company and sector which adopted Disruptive Innovation Strategy has been taken.

3. The period of study was from 2016 (Launch of Reliance Jio) to 2022.

4. To achieve the research objective this research is conducted and confined only to the impact of disruption in two big telecom circle of the country i.e. Uttar Pradesh East and Uttar Pradesh West.

5. Data has been collected from the population / cellular network users of UP East and UP West only.

6. The researcher did this study in a limited amount of time and based it on how Jio changed things after it came into the market. This means that the study's scope is quite small.

7. There are small number of studies on disruptive innovation has been conducted. But this study is probably new in its own right when it comes to the telecom industry and the case of Reliance Jio.

HYPOTHESIS

Hypothesis is formation of certain assumption before the starting of research or investigation. It is often called "Pre-test assumptions." During the research process, the hypothesis has been tested and either accepted or rejected based on how the collected data and findings were analysed. The goal of this study was to check the following theory:

1. (H_{01}) Disruptive Innovation Strategy has no difference from Evolutionary and Revolutionary Innovation Strategy

2. (H_{02}) Disruptive Innovation has no effect on new market and new product or services.

3. (H_{03}) Indian Telecom Sector is not affected by Disruptive Innovation Strategy.

4. (H_{04}) There is no impact of disruption on overall business of Jio Infocomm Ltd.

LIMITATION OF THE STUDY

1. This study was limited to only Indian Telecom sector largely focus on Reliance Jio Infocomm Ltd and not significantly to other market players.

2. The sample for the present study comprised of units from a comparatively small section of society. A more diverse sample comprising of respondents from different religions, regions, castes and classes may have provided with more confidently generalisable results.

3. Respondents' biasness was the biggest challenge as well as limitation to the study.

4. The sample size is confined to 250 respondents only due to time and cost limitation.

5. A total of 300 questionnaires were sent to the respondents in which 250 have responded correctly and in valid form.

6. This research is conducted in the two big telecom circle of the country i.e. Uttar Pradesh East and Uttar Pradesh West. Therefore, the conclusion may not be generalised to the other telecom circle/ state/ country or geographical regions.

7. It was not possible to explain certain points related to the questions of the questionnaire to all the respondents, So, the respondents may misinterpret it.

8. For some personal reasons, respondents may not wish to disclose some information and may answer some questions superficially.

9. There may still be the possibility of adding some new dimensions of some variables to the existing dimensions, affecting the customers' perception and expectations towards innovation in the telecom sector and the disruption.

10. There is the possibility of occurring errors in the collection of the sample, collecting responses from the respondent, and interpretation of the collected responses.

11. Customers of all four telecom service providers were chosen, out of which maximum responses were given by Jio users. Therefore, the generalization of the finding should be considered carefully.

12. In addition to the above, the statistical analysis carried out and the tools and techniques applied in this study have their restrictions.

13. This research is specially focused on mobile telecom services to get the required outcome.

RESEARCH DESIGN

The research design is how a research problem is put together as a whole. It is the overall plan you make for putting the different parts of the study together in a way that makes sense. It is a plan or guide for how the research will be done. In simple terms, it is an outline of how you will do your research. **Smith (1976)** says, "A design is a carefully thought-out plan for how to carry out an experiment. Design of an experiment refers to the selection as well as arrangement of condition. Kerlinger says, "Research design is the plan, structure, and strategy of an investigation made so that answers to research questions can be found and variation is kept to a minimum." A research design is a plan for studying a scientific problem in a systematic way. A research design is how the conditions for collecting and analysing data are set up in a way that aims to be both relevant to the research goal and cost-effective. The type of research design used in this study is both quantitative and descriptive.

- **Descriptive Research Design:** Surveys and other fact-finding questions of different kinds are used in descriptive research. The main goal of descriptive research is to describe how things are at the time of the study. In social science and business research, the term "ex post facto research" frequently refers to the descriptive research studies. This method is different from others because the researcher has little or no control over the variables. He or she only has to tell what is going on or what has happened. Most ex post facto research projects are descriptive studies wherein the researcher looks at things like consumer preferences, how often they buy things, how often they shop, etc. Even though the researchers can't control the variables, they may still try to find out what caused the chosen problem in ex post facto studies. When doing descriptive research, different kinds of survey methods, as well as correlational and comparative methods, are used.

- **Quantitative Research:** Quantitative research looks at things that can be measured or put in terms of numbers. It involves figuring out how much or how much something is. In this kind of research, different statistical and economic methods are used to analyse the data. Which includes things like correlation, regression, time series analysis, and so on.

POPULATION OF THE STUDY

A population is the total number of people in a group, whether that group is a country or a group of people with something in common. In statistics, a population is the set of people from which a study's statistical sample is taken. So, a population is a group of people who are put together by something they have in common. A sample can also mean a part of a population that is statistically important, not the whole population. Because of this, a data analysis of a sample should report the standard error, or standard deviation, of the results from the whole population. Only an analysis of an entire population would have no standard error. All the telecom users of the Uttar Pradesh (UP East & UP West) have been taken as population for the study.

SAMPLING METHOD AND SAMPLING UNIT

The sampling method is the process of gathering information about a population and figuring out what that information means. It's the way that data is collected, and the sample space is very big. In this study Non- Probabilistic Convenience sampling method used to collect the data from the end consumers of Reliance Jio and its competitors through questionnaire. For this purpose, total 300 responses were collected from consumers of Jio and other telecom operators using 4G network as well as 3G and 2G also. Out of which 250 responses were found valid for the further research and analysis.

SOURCES OF DATA

1. **Primary Data:** Large portion study was based on the primary data. The survey method was employed; the well-structured questionnaire was designed to gather information from the customers of various telecom service providers of Uttar Pradesh to analyse and build the relationship among the dependent and independent variables.

2. **Secondary Data:** The secondary data has been arranged from various published materials like various reports or TRAI, DOT, Govt. of India and other reports, newspapers, articles, journals, books, magazines, various websites, internet and other government records etc.

RELIABILITY AND VALIDITY OF RESEARCH INSTRUMENT

A questionnaire is one of the most common ways to get information for research, especially in the social sciences. In research, the main goal of a questionnaire is to get relevant information in the most reliable and valid way. Validity and reliability are two important parts of research methodology that have to do with how accurate and consistent a survey or questionnaire is. Validity and reliability are related, but they don't mean the same thing. A measurement doesn't have to be valid to be reliable. But if a measurement is correct, it is usually also accurate.

1. **RELIABILITY**

   It means how often a method measures something the same way. The measurement is regarded as reliable if it always leads to the same result when the same methods are used in the same situations. For a test to be valid, it has to be reliable. The results of the reliability analysis used Cronbach's alpha, which is another name for the coefficient alpha, to measure how similar the items were. In this study the *Cronbach's alpha is 0.844*, which indicates that a high level of internal consistency for the scale with this specific sample. (Detail mentioned in Chapter 5 Later On)

2. **VALIDITY**

Validity in research surveys has to do with how well the survey measures the right things that need to be measured. In simple words, validity is how well an instrument measures what it is supposed to measure. Validity is a measure of how well the data collected covers the real area of study (Ghauri and Gronhaug, 2005). Validity means, basically, "measure what is meant to be measured" (Field, 2005).

<u>Validity Analysis</u>

Based on the validity analysis output in mind some values like Pearson Correlation or Correlation value between of the different items or the item with the total score also known as Sig. (2-tailed) was significant level of 5%, while N is the total survey respondents is 250 people. As explained in the validity analysis and based on the significant value obtained by the Sig. (2-tailed) of 0.000 in the case of maximum items of the questionnaire is <0.05, so it can be concluded that all items was valid. (Detail mentioned in Chapter 5 Later on and Data table attached in Appendices.

02

DISRUPTIVE INNOVATION STRATEGIES

Disruptive innovation refers to innovation that transforms expensive or highly sophisticated products or services—previously accessible to a high-end or more-skilled segment of consumers—to those that are more affordable and accessible to a broader population. This transition causes a market disruption by replacing mature, well-established competitors.

M.A. Sikandar (2019). The notion is very true that, new things out of date the old ones. Despite its being a relatively new concept, disruptive innovation has a notable past. Consider the progression of plastic from natural materials like shellac, from chemically processed materials like cellulose and natural rubber, to contemporary polymers like Bakelite and polyethylene, etc., which are substituting metals in a variety of applications in the market. When it comes to business models, strategies, services, and other aspects of the market, disruptive innovation has really been considered as a change agent. An overall disruptive shift contributes to the creation of a new marketplace with new competitors, demand patterns, and usage patterns.

Disruptive Innovation

(Twin, 2022) Disruptive innovation is not an act of enhancing or improving products for a particular target population; rather, it is concerned with the technology utilised to make them simple to use and accessible to a broader, non-targeted market. The emergence of digital music downloads, which have mostly displaced compact discs (CDs), is a good example of disruptive innovation.

Clayton Christensen pioneered the concept of disruptive innovation in his book 'The Innovator's Solution', the follow-up to his 1997 book 'The Innovator's Dilemma'. Christensen hypothesised that businesses engage with two kinds of technology. Sustainable technologies are ones that allow a company to progressively enhance its operations over a certain period of time. These technologies and the manner in which they were implemented in the company were created largely to enable corporations to stay competitive, or at the very least, to maintain the status quo. The disruptive technologies and the manner in which they were incorporated—the disruptive innovations—were more difficult to plan for and possibly more damaging to businesses that did not give them adequate consideration.

Investing in a disruptive innovation is difficult. Rather than focusing on the advancement of the technology itself, an investor must consider how firms will react to disruptive technologies. Google (GOOGL), Amazon (AMZN) and Meta (FB) previously Facebook, are examples of corporations that have placed a significant emphasis on the internet as a disruptive technology. Companies that failed to incorporate disruptive innovation into their strategic planning have been pushed aside since the internet has become so pervasive in the modern world. Artificial intelligence and its capacity to learn from people and execute their tasks may soon be a game-changing breakthrough for the whole labour market.

What constitutes a technology or invention "disruptive" is debatable. This word may be applied to technologies that are not genuinely disruptive. The Internet was disruptive since it was not an evolution of prior technologies. It was something novel that generated never-before-seen models for producing money. Other business strategies clearly suffered as a result of this.

People utilising smartphones rather than laptops and desktops for personal computing requirements, such as online surfing & streaming, is another illustration of disruptive innovation. These functions are supported by miniature processors, chips, and software programmes that have been made possible by technological advances. Smartphone developers addressed the vast market of mobile customers with cellular devices that find it cumbersome to carry and use computers when surfing the web. Smartphones are compact, readily portable and storable, and relatively inexpensive compared to desktops and laptops.

In contrast, the Model T car is not seen as a typical example of disruptive innovation due to the fact that it was an upgrade on an existing technology that was not widely embraced upon its debut. The automobile industry did not take off until mass manufacturing lowered costs and shifted the whole transportation system from horses to wheels. In this regard, the mass-production system meets the requirements for disruptive innovation.

Example of Amazon

The way the bookselling business was changed by the internet is a perfect illustration of how the internet's innovations can be disruptive. Amazon (AMZN) beat out the big bookselling chains because it could show its stock without having to have a store in every town and ship the book to the customer's house. Before online purchasing became very popular, people bought books in conventional bookshops.

Amazon's profits as well as market share grew in line with its popularity, putting many bookstores out of business or on the back shelf. Since its start, Amazon has been able to utilise the internet to establish a platform for online shopping. Most of what you can buy in a store, including groceries, can be purchased from Amazon's website. And it all started with a small company that started in a garage and used the potential of the internet to meet the needs of an online shopping niche market.

Example of Netflix

Netflix is another company that is shaking things up. At a time when there were a lot of video stores where you could rent VHS tapes and

DVDs, Netflix saw an opportunity to serve an untapped market of online customers. Using the rising potential of the internet, they gave customers the chance to look through their library of DVDs, rent what they wanted without worrying about someone else renting the same thing, and have their choices sent straight to their homes.

Not long after they started renting DVDs by mail, they changed their business model and found a way to shake up the market by streaming entertainment online. But now, Netflix's competitors have been able to successfully copy this business model, which hurts Netflix's market share. It's time and the market that will show how long Netflix can stay on top, but there's no question that they caused a big disruption in the market. After Netflix changed the media business, Blockbuster reduced its number from more than 9,000 stores to just one, which is now known as Airbnb.

Requirements for Disruptive Innovation

For disruptive innovation to happen, it's important to have access to markets that are being overlooked or ignored, as well as technology that can make a product accessible and cheaper. For a new business model to be disruptive, the chain of partners, such as suppliers, contractors, and distributors, must also benefit from it. Certain essential requirements include:

Enabling Technology: In respect of business, it is explained as any technology or innovation that considerably changes or improves the operations or how the peoples do the things. In the context of disruptive innovation, a "enabling technology" is an innovation or technology that makes it possible for a product to be affordable and available to a larger market. Basically, how quickly a market can really be shaken up varies based on how quickly new technology is made and then improved. But the pace of the disruption isn't always a good way to measure how well the disruption is working.

Innovative Business Model: An innovative business model is one that utilises innovations to attract potential or low-tier customers. Most of the time, these groups don't help established companies make money or buy their products because they can't afford them or because the products are too complicated for them to use. This business model, which incumbents didn't pick up on because the disruptor's initial profit margins were low, aims to offer cheap, easy-to-use solutions.

Coherent Value Network: The downstream and upstream business partners that stand to gain from a successful disruption are part of the coherent value network. To adapt to or fit into the new business model, the suppliers, distributors, and vendors may need to change their processes or reorganise. For the network not to fail, members must agree toward the new business model. If you don't disrupt old network processes, you'll end up with results that aren't what you wanted.

Disruptive Innovation Vs. Sustaining Innovation

A disruptive innovation is one that makes products and services easier to use and cheaper in markets that aren't desired or aren't being paid attention to. Established companies usually try to enhance their goods and services to satisfy their most profitable customers, ignoring the desires and needs of untapped segments. This lack of attention makes it possible for smaller companies or newcomers to target this ignored group with easier, cheaper options.

Sustaining innovation, on the other side, is the process of coming up with new ways to make products and services effective for customers who already use them. This can be done based on what customers or the market want. Sustaining innovation isn't about going after untapped or ignored markets. Instead, it's about coming up with new ideas to stay relevant and competitive. Making CDs that can hold a lot of music and don't get scratched is a way for CD makers to keep coming up with new ideas. It is a disruptive innovation for a company to offer digital downloads over the internet, causing CDs obsolete.

The Bottom Line

Disruptive innovation is the use of new ways to make products and services easy to use and affordable for people who haven't been able to buy them in the past or for customers who were traditionally unmarketable. Unlike sustainable innovation, it doesn't involve making products better for customers who already have them.

For disruptive innovation to work, you need technology that can make the product or service cheaper and easier to use, a business model that endorses disruptive innovation; and the network of downstream and upstream partners who support the disruption and will benefit from its success. "Disruptive innovation is the process of making a product, service, or offering that is expensive or complicated into one that is relatively simple, cheaper, and available to a wider group of people. It shows how technology and innovation can transform markets by making solutions that are cheap, easy to use, and widely available. When this happens, the new market disrupts the old one."

Review of Literature

A review of the literature is a synopsis of a field of research that points out specific study questions. For a literature review, you have to summarise and evaluate a wide range of sources, such as research articles, books, and online content from professional and scholarly journals. The inquiry for literature assists in locating data and other resources that are useful. Search engines can be used to look for things on the Web and in a bibliography database. Theoretical constructs might be a helpful way to learn more about a certain subject area. Scanning, taking notes, framing the literature review, writing the literature review, and making a bibliography are all parts of making a literature review.

The goal of the review of the literature is to show that the author has read and understood the most important published work on a certain topic or question in a certain area. The whole work can be carried out from any source, including online or offline sources. It could be an individual assignment or part of a report, thesis, or dissertation. Specifically, the review will be based on the research objectives or statements made by the issue, and it can help the researcher plan their next steps.

This chapter briefly discusses the literature available in the area chosen for the study. The scope of the review of literature is divided into two sections for the holistic study:

Section 1: Review of Literature of Disruptive Innovation Strategy.

Section 2: Review of Literature of Disruptive Innovation in Indian Telecom Sector by Reliance Jio.

Section 1: Review of Literature of Disruptive Innovation Strategy

Tushman and Anderson (1986) conclude that discontinuous change can happen in both products and procedures and also that discontinuous innovations fall on a spectrum from radical change that isn't necessarily disruptive to major paradigm shifts that are disruptive for entire value networks.

(Tushman & Nadler, 1986) It has been established that radical innovation consists of applying significant new technologies or significant new combos of technologies to new market opportunities. This leads to new products, services, or business models that can be built into disruptive value networks.

Veryzer (1988) makes a distinction between "product capability," which is how customers and users see the benefits of a product, and "technological capability," which is how much the product expands capabilities beyond the boundaries of the organisation. He had shown that organisations could provide three different kinds of breaks, which are shown in the figure below. Once more, the perceived value of a product or service is important for discontinuities that could lead to disruptive innovations, and each type of discontinuity needs a different way to manage it.

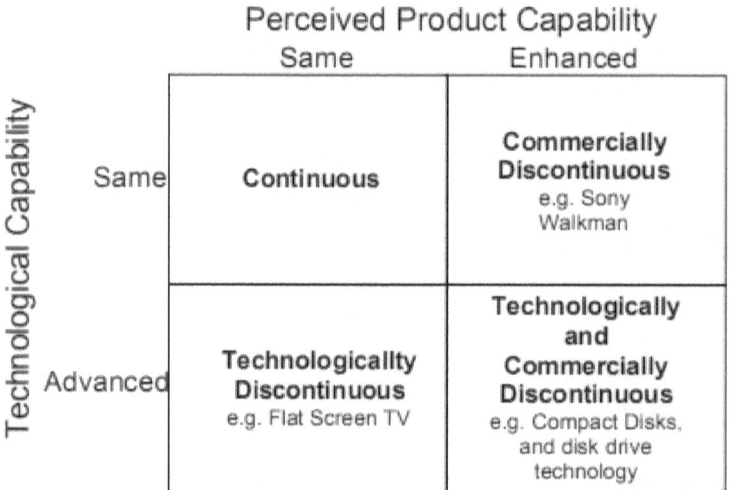

Figure 2.1

Source: *Types of Discontinuous Innovation (Veryzer, 1998)*

(Christensen's 1997) original theory was about disruptive technologies. Over time, the same theory has been utilised to describe all types of disruptive innovations. This was a mistake. Different types of innovations have different impacts on competition and lead to different types of markets. They should be looked at as separate things. This article is a summary of what the academic literature says about two types of disruptive innovation: radical product innovations and business-model innovations. It says that even though they are similar to what Christensen calls "disruptive innovations" in a lot of ways, they still are different things: they create different types of markets, give established companies very different problems to solve; and have very different effects on managers. Progress can only be made on the theme of disruptive innovation when it is broken down into such smaller groups.

In his study, **Christensen's (1997)** was mostly about technological innovation and how new technologies beat out technologies that seemed to be better in the market. Over time, Christensen expanded the concept of the term "integrated" to include business models and products as well as technologies.

Christensen and Raynor (2003) say that discount department stores, low-cost point-to-point airlines, cheap mass-market products like power tools, photo copiers, and motorcycles, and online businesses like bookselling, brokerage, education, and travel agents are all examples of disruptive innovations. Even though he agrees that all such innovations are indeed a threat to the status quo, treating them all as the same has made things a lot more confusing. A disruptive technological innovation is very different from such a disruptive business model innovation and a disruptive product innovation. These innovations come about in different ways, affect competition in different ways, and require incumbents to respond in different ways. Putting all kinds of disruptive innovations into the same category is like putting apples and oranges together. This will make it hard to study disruptive innovations in the coming years **(Henderson and Clark, 1990).**

Hamel (2000) says that the potential benefits of "non-linear" or "disruptive" innovation could be found at the level of the whole system. He says that companies can come up with services or products that are disruptive, but their real worth is only unlocked when the whole system is taken into account. Hamel says that "Business Concept Innovation" happens when the business model is broken down and exposed to disruptive thinking. He says that this is the true purpose of revolutionary innovation, as it shakes up ideas, markets, and entire value networks. In short, revolutionary innovations fall on a continuum from "radical incrementalism," which brings major changes to the mainstream market and is mostly competence-enhancing with low environmental turbulence and low market uncertainty, to "disruptive innovations," which bring major changes to the mainstream market and its valuation attributes and are mostly competence-destroying with high environmental turbulence and high market uncertainty.

(Thomond, P., and Lettice, F. (2002) came up with a functional definition and features of disruptive innovation: "A disruptive innovation is an effectively used product, service, or business model that significantly changes the needs and wants of a mainstream market and disrupts its former main players."

It has the following characteristics:

- It begins its success by satisfying the unfulfilled needs of an emerging or niche market.
- Its set of performance characteristics, which are highly valued by niche market customers, were not initially valued by mainstream markets. Customers in the main market and competitors in the same market value different sets of performance attributes, so they both think the innovation isn't good enough.
- When a product, service, or business model is used in a niche market, investments can be made to improve its performance. Then, it can create or enter new niche markets to get more customers.
- As people learn more about the product, service, or business model, the mainstream market is forced to reconsider what it values.
- The change in how the mainstream market sees and values what it values is what sparks innovation and allows for the disruption and replacement of mainstream products, services, or business models.

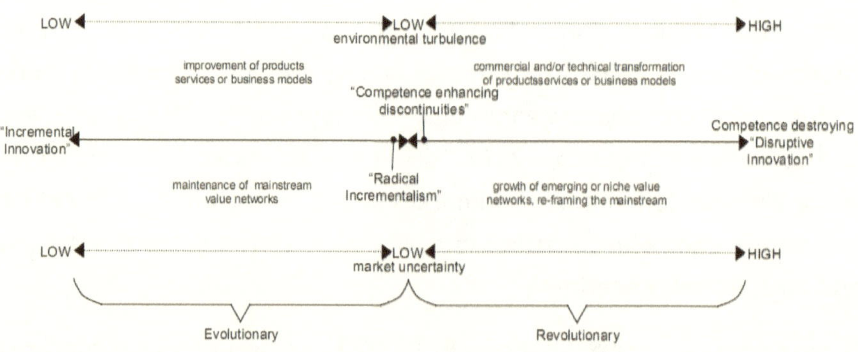

Figure 2.2

Source: *Innovation Continuum (Thomond, P., & Lettice, F. (2002)*

Charitou and Markides (2003) have demonstrated that incumbent firms have a number of options when deciding how to respond to disruptive business model innovations. The majority of these, including the "disrupt the disruptor" strategy used by companies like Swatch, do add value.

Danneels (2004) examined the theory underneath disruptive technological innovation & came up with a list of questions that need to be looked into more deeply. One of these problems is what disruptive innovation really means. Although both managers and educationalists use the term "disruptive innovation" a lot, it seems that there is still a lack of understanding of what it means.

Markides and Geroski (2005) wrote about how big companies could use these kinds of new products to their advantage. Their argument is that big companies shouldn't even try to come up with these kinds of innovations. Instead, they should leave it to small, new companies that have the right skills and mindset to succeed in this game. Instead, firms that are already well-known should focus on what they do best: turn small markets into large and global markets.

Yu, D., and Hang, C. C.'s (2010) research, they tried to bring together and talk about the most recent arguments about the Disruptive Innovation theory, as well as to raise questions for more research. The most important issues have been summed up in three main ways: (1) "What is disruptive technology and disruptive innovation," including how it has changed over time, what it is, and what it means. (2) "How to use the theory to make predictions" and (3) "How to make a possible disruptive innovation possible." There is a trend to use the marketing literature's wealth of knowledge and tools to study how to find new markets and meet customers' unmet needs. The technology perspective got very little attention, and a lot of research is needed to figure out how to make candidate technologies for disruptive innovation on purpose. As a "take-away" for managers, there is also a list of things that could stop or help disruptive innovation.

Baatartogtokh, B., and King, A. A., (2015), identified four key parts of the principle of disruption: (i) that incumbents in a business are improving along a path of sustaining innovation; (ii) that they overshoot customer needs; (iii) that they have the ability to react to disruptive threats; and (iv) that incumbents end up struggling because of the disruption.

(Petzold et al., 2019) add to the literature on disruptive innovation in three ways with their study. First, they show how the process view gives a dynamic perspective of disruptive innovation by combining what we already know about events and actions that lead to a disruptive effect over the time with what we already know about the process view. They suggested that the disruptive innovation process takes place in three stages: the initiation phase, the niche market phase, and the mainstream market phase. The dynamics of each phase are affected by (1) how the opportunity and the entrant's innovation are seen and what expectations there are for them, (2) the entrant's strategy, and (3) how the entrant uses enabling technologies and factor markets. Second, they put these findings into a process model, taking into account the multi-temporal dynamics of the process. This shows that there are many different paths that could lead people away from a disruptive path (shown as "missed opportunities of disruptive innovation") if they are not managed well. Third, because they saw disruptive innovation as a process that changes over time, they described the procedure in terms of (a) the timing of entrance and underlying processes, which influences (b) the synchronisation of actions and events which is shaped by (c) the ability to adopt strategic actions.

Assink, M. (2006) found in his study that many large companies don't come up with innovations that shake things up. It is said that the main things that make it hard to make a successful disruptive innovation are a few inhibiting factors. These factors include the inability to unlearn old mental models, an effective dominant design or business idea, a risk-averse corporate climate, poor innovation process management, a lack of follow-through skills, and the inability to develop new ideas. The concept of a disruptive innovation capability model makes it easier to see how all of these factors affect each other. There is still a huge gap between what people want to do and what they can do in terms of disruptive innovation. As a company grows, it should be a key part of its growth strategy to develop unique skills that can help close this gap.

The Power to Disrupt (2010): E-Content by Site Core Company, whose expert team creates extremely relevant e-resources on the latest developments in marketing and consumer experience, says that a disruptive company is one that interacts with its customers in a humanistic way. The founder of 650 Labs, Mark Zawacki, says that being a disruptive company is different from being an innovative company. A disruptive company cares a lot about its customers and thinks that their needs, wants, and expectations are all in sync. In the process of meeting this loop of needs, wants, and expectations, these companies will create a new market. When disruptive companies sell products, services, or ideas, they connect with people on an emotional and sometimes spiritual level. These disruptive brands line up with the dreams, ideals, and values of their customers, and the services or products they offer are just a way to get the customer to the level of dreams, ideals, and values they want.

Michael E. Raynor (2011) says that disruptive innovation is about how new start-ups or new organisations are giving established players in a sector a hard time. They sell better-quality products for less money, and they fill the needs of market segments that the big players would have ignored by not making their products more sophisticated. Over time, these newcomers get better at what they do, so they can compete with the big players and win over their customers.

Christensen (2015) wrote an article about it because more and more people were using it without understanding what it really meant. At the same time, disruption's use was only found outside of technology, which is where it was first used, and reasons were given to re-explain it. The meaning of disruptive innovation, as well as the definitions of "disruption" and "disruptor," came from the literature. A disruptive innovation is one that creates a "blue ocean" market that eventually shakes up an existing market, displacing firms, products, and alliances that were already there.

Ahluwalia, S., Mahto, R. V., and Walsh, S. T. (2017) describe how a region went from having few resources to having a lot of them. Innovation is a way to move from a situation of lack to one of plenty. If market resources and social structure can tell if an innovation will work or not, having a lot of social capital doesn't help with disruptive innovation. Oversupply reduces the potential for entrepreneurial development. In this paper, the author gives one such conceptual framework to help explain and comprehend the relationship between the ideas of scarcity, abundance, and innovation from the point of view of the market. This paper talks about the necessity of knowing how radical or disruptive innovations happen to make the world a better place and what market conditions drive innovators, especially in places like the Bottom Billion and the shrinking middle class, where there is poverty and a lack of resources. The authors use arguments from the theory of social capital, the theory of disruptive innovation and entrepreneurial action, as well as the theory of social innovation to construct a theoretical model of disruptive innovation in an environment with few resources.

Roy, R., and Islam, M. (2017) have looked into how a group of new companies that use technology that is eventually disrupted come up with new products. The research article is mostly about two types of newcomers: those who have relevant experience in disrupted technology and those who don't. By using the industrial robotics industry as a case study, the authors of our study look at product innovation utilising disrupted technology during two different time periods: the first, before sales of disruptive products really took off, and the second, after they did. The authors find that the two types of new entrants did not differ in how innovative their products were before their sales took off. However, firms with expertise in disrupted technology made more innovative goods after their sales took off. The research shows that the limits of the usefulness of past experience are more complicated than what the literature says. It has an effect on product innovation only after sales take off, when uncertainty about demand is low.

Christensen, C. M., McDonald, R., Altman, E. J., and Palmer, J. E. (2018) wrote an article that tried to update and change the way people usually think about disruptive innovation and to point out places where more research could be done. We've shown how a descriptive account of how technology changes turned into a normative theory of creativity and competitive response. We've also shown how recent additions and changes to the theory's main ideas have made them stronger and more useful, and we've suggested good directions for future research. We hope to re-energize the research literature on disruption as a theoretical approach by giving it a new, unified theoretical and conceptual basis and the start of a new research programme. We don't want this paper to be the last word on disruptive innovation. Instead, we want it to be the start of a new line of research.

Urbinati et al. (2019) wrote a paper about how incumbents change their management styles over time to deal with the threat posed by waves of disruptive innovations that happen over the course of an industry's lifecycle. This is an important question to look into in the field of disruptive innovations, to see if and how the development and application of different management approaches follow or don't follow a path that changes over time when incumbents are faced with a steady flow of disruptive innovations in the industry where they work.

Modawski, W. (2019), breaks down one of the best examples of a cutting-edge digital business model that is disrupting so many industries and transforming the way individuals live. They are Spotify, Netflix, Airbnb, Uber, Revolut, and Amazon. Second, it gives a brief history of the technologies that got us to this point, focusing on the development of the computer system, the internet, and smartphones, as well as the key ideas used to describe these businesses, such as the business model and disruptive innovation. It also gives an in-depth look at the economic and legal problems these businesses have to deal with. At the end of the research, new technologies were shown that, if everyone used them, could lead to new major business models that change the way things are done.

Travica, B. (Ed.) (2019), talked more about the pros and cons of the technology or innovation disruption theory. The theory has gained some support, and people who work in information systems and other fields have started using the word "disruption" to describe new technologies. This talk looks at parts of the theory and how they apply to digital technologies and the company Uber. The results show that the theory is not complete and needs to be worked on more. The next steps for research are mapped out. The author says that words like "disrupt" should be used with care. Even though business and data systems strategy theory needs to move forward with new ideas, the fact that it's easy to explain and predict things right away shouldn't be confused with good science and management. The theory of disruptive innovation needs to be worked on further before it can be used to move theory and practise forward.

Guo, J., et al (2019), in their study, they tried to come up with a quantitative framework for measuring disruptive innovations based on their many different features. The goal of this study is to add to the discussion about the ex-ante approaches that try to find disruptive innovations. Based on a systematic review of the literature and conceptual frameworks, ten indicators are made up of three types of multidimensionality: technological features, market dynamics, and the external environment. These indicators show how innovations have many different aspects. Then, a few of the indicators are linked together, and the weight of each indicator is based on how well it is linked.

Mukhopadhyay, S., and Whalley, J. (2021), in their research shed light on this phenomenon by analysing the rise of Jio Platform, an India-based green-field platform that offers mobile and electronic services. Their analysis shows what the disruptor did to deal with the problems that the established companies and their own advanced technology posed. They showed that the disruptive entrant took three strategic steps to get out of its "disruptor's dilemma": active market development for complementary products, using powerful complements as force multipliers, and making good use of framing to get legitimacy and support.

Section 2: Review of Literature of Disruptive Innovation in Indian Telecom Sector by Reliance Jio

McClellan, S., Low, S., and Tan, W. T. (2004), inside this research study, the authors looked at the most important architectural, market, and technological issues related to "disruptive technologies," which are changing the way global telecommunications are built and run. The author tries to group and highlight some of the most important technologies, channels, and services that are affecting how telecommunications networks are changing. Many of these functional parts came about because customers asked for them and because "legacy services" were re-defined in the context of packet-based capabilities (or limitations). In this context, the authors looked at service quality in packet-switched networks, commoditization of operating systems, hardware, and access bandwidth, as well as some key protocols that affect the structure and functioning of telephony networks.

Latzer, M. (2009) explains why certain approaches are useful and how they can be used in the convergent telecom/communication sector. He focused on the concept of disruption, which is a relatively new way to tell the difference between sustaining and disruptive innovations, and looked at how it fits in with other types of innovation theory. According to the research, there are a lot of disruptive changes in the area of internet protocol-based innovations that combine with wireless technology. When one looks more closely, he/she can see that these classifications and ratings are not only different in small ways, but they also contradict each other. The article discusses these differences by talking about how analysts who use the disruption concept have to make hard decisions. It says that it isn't very useful in the convergent communications industry and also that single-firm assessments can't be used to make broad claims. In his conceptual paper,

Kalyani (2016) used SWOT analysis. She found that Jio was a successful project because it got the right mix of the 7 Ps of service marketing: product, place, price, promotion, physical evidence, process, and people; got rid of paper work in the subscription process; and could offer cheap phones with fast data. Reliance Jio did very well with its advertising campaigns by focusing on the younger generation and getting good word of mouth.

Biswarup Chatterjee (2017) quotes Christensen Clayton, who said, "Disruptive innovation is not limited to technology; it can also be about a product, process, method, company, brand, or repair." The paper talks about how Reliance Jio has forced companies like Vodafone, Airtel, Idea, and others to modify their marketing strategies and services. Reliance Jio was able to shake up the market and win the hearts of customers in a very short amount of time. The study showed that when Indians buy telecom services, the most important things to them are still a low price, a good network, good customer service, and ease of use.

Medhi (2017) focused on finding out why telecom users carry another operator as a secondary network. She found that most users were very happy with Jio's services, but there was room for improvement in terms of coverage of networks and call connectivity.

Laddha and Trivedi (2017) employed a total of six factors to figure out how people feel about a brand. These are personality, culture, usage of attributes, benefits, and values. It was decided that Jio is doing well in areas like value, culture, personality, and usage, but that the product and benefits need to be improved.

Mahalaxmi and Kumar (2017) came to the conclusion that there was no significant link between respondents' income and which telecom operator they preferred. They also found that about 97% of respondents were happy with Reliance Jio's services, and most of them were teenagers or students. They have also come to the conclusion that the marketing strategies and promotional offers used by Jio had a big impact on how customers behaved.

Chinthala, Madhuri, and Kumar (2017) came to the conclusion that most of the people who took part in the study were happy with

Reliance Jio's services, especially the internet. Also, there is no big difference in how satisfied people are based on whether they are male or female. In the end, they came to the conclusion that many customers have complained about poor customer service.

Salomi and Selvan's (2017) showed that companies are concentrating on penetration strategies because there is more competitive pressure in the telecom industry. Reliance Jio was the first to do this. The most important goal of

Boobalan and Jayaraman's (2017) study was to find the problems with Reliance Jio and recommend ways to fix them. They came to the conclusion that 41% and 36% of respondents were happy with Reliance Jio's services and knew about them. They also came to the conclusion that there is a strong link between users' income and how happy they are with the service, but not between users' age and how aware they are of the service.

Singh (2017) says that Reliance Jio's low-cost data plans as well as free services have had a major effect on the telecom industry. The competitors' sales have dropped by a lot, which has led to closures or mergers in the telecom industry. One of the main reasons Reliance Jio was so successful because it advertised so much.

Brahmani and Vamsi (2017) used the Shapiroh-Wilk test, the one-sample t-test, the two-sample t-test, and the ANOVA in the R 3.2.5 package to analyse and explain the data. Cost-effectiveness, free calls, no roaming charges, free channels, free caller tunes, and voice clarity were cited as the main reasons why customers were more satisfied. On the other hand, internet speed, compatibility with other SIM cards, and voice call connectivity were cited as reasons why customers were less satisfied.

Sisili et al. (2018) looked at connectivity, customer service, speed, getting new connections, and compatibility as ways to measure customer satisfaction. A study revealed that a lot of users were happy with Jio's services, that include free local as well as national SMS, coverage outside, roaming service, error-free SMS delivery and receipt, and fast internet.

Santosh and Rajandran (2018) focused on Reliance Jio's service quality, how well it worked, how much it cost, and how many free services it offered to figure out how customers felt about it. The study comes to the conclusion that there is a strong link between level of income and level of satisfaction, but not between age and level of awareness. Also, advertising and the availability of free plans were among the most important things that made customers satisfied and the study also said that there was an urgent need to improve call blocking, call drop, setting of the service stations, speed, and coverage area.

Lonare et al. (2018) focused on the likely reasons why customers switched to Jio, the company's marketing strategies, and how the revenue streams of other telecom companies changed before and after Reliance Jio came out. Price, the value of the brand, the speed of data, the quality of voice calls, and customer service have been mentioned as independent variables. Also, it was decided that other service providers' income dropped by a lot after Jio came out. Customers switched to Jio because of three main things: their monthly costs, the plans that Reliance Jio offered, and also the effect of promotional work. Aside from that, authors have pointed to Jio's "penetration pricing strategy" as a main reason for its large market share growth.

Patlolla and Doodipala (2018) found that the launch of Jio has made a big difference in how customers know about it and how happy they are with it. They also found that the network coverage needs to be improved. Also, it was seen that many subscribers are using Airtel as their main network and Jio as their secondary network just to get faster data.

Joy and Bahl (2018) By analysing the data from TRAI Analytics Portal they glanced at how customers were satisfied based on the speed of 4G data, call quality and experience. Reliance Jio's plans fell under three main categories: disrupting the market, disrupting prices, and changing the way things are done. The study found that 78% of people were happy with the quality and experience of their calls.

Indumathy and Velmurugan (2018) study of Reliance Jio looked at things like usage of SIM, data, calling service, and other services to figure out how customers like them and how happy they are. They have come to the conclusion that Jio is the second network of choice for many users because it has better data services. It was also seen that there is a strong link between demographic factors like age and occupation and how people like their services. Users were very happy with Reliance Jio's data service, calling service, plans, and offers, but the call connectivity and network coverage need to be improved.

Daga, Chandra, and Malik (2018) looked at how Reliance Jio and the government helped digitise India and change how the Indian telecommunications sector is set up. A study showed that Jio has changed the lives of its subscribers by offering cheap and affordable rate plans. It was also said that respondents believe that the government's work on "Digital India" has helped the Indian telecommunications sector make big steps toward becoming digital.

Russell, C. L. (2018) in his article, the author looked at necessary electromagnetic frequencies, exposure standards, and current scientific literature about the health effects of 2G, 3G, and 4G exposure, as well as some of the existing literature on 5G frequencies. The question of what is a public health problem will be brought up, as well as the need to move forward with new wireless technologies with cautious. To power the Internet of Things (IoT), a new generation of even short higher frequency 5G wavelengths is on the way. With a huge 5G communications network, the Internet of Things (IoT) promises to make our lives easier and more convenient. However, the growth of broadband with shorter wavelengths of radio frequency radiation raises concerns about health and safety. There is still debate about whether 2G, 3G, or 4G wireless technologies cause harm. The effects of 5G technologies on people and the environment have been studied much less. People say that adding this high frequency 5G radio waves to an existing complicated mix of lower frequencies will have a negative effect on both the mental and physical health of the public.

(Joy, T., & Bahl, S., 2018), in its research article titled "Impact of Reliance Jio on Indian Telecom Industry," talked about how Reliance Jio changed the telecom industry by making people use their phones a lot more, which grew the market, pushed out old-school competitors, and made customers more satisfied. We talk about the new strategies that Reliance Jio used to get a hold of the Indian market, and we try to figure out how happy customers are as a whole. During the course of the study, an exploratory research method is used and TRIA data has been used as secondary source for the study. The results show that Reliance Jio has changed the way the telecom market works as a whole. Their strategies have made Jio the fourth largest telecom service provider in less than two years, and they have built a customer base that is loyal and happy. The paper also looks at Reliance Jio's different features and some of the ways it has an advantage over other telecom operators.

Schneir et al. (2019) mentioned in their research as how different things affect the business case for a 5G network. The study was done for the years 2020–2030 in three boroughs in central London, UK. The results show that it would be good for business for a 5G network to only offer mobile broadband services. Return on investment can be negative if traffic and costs are much higher than expected and sales are growing more slowly than expected. The sensitivity analysis indicates that return on investment goes down when both traffic and costs are much higher than our baseline forecasts and sales don't grow as fast as we thought they would. Sharing networks helps enhance the business case in a big way. More research needs to be done to figure out the business case on a local or national scale and for a network that offers more services than just broadband.

Gupta, Raghav, and Dhakad (2019) came to the conclusion that Jio has made the competition the most fierce it has ever been. Some of the rivals had to join forces, and others had to modify their plans and start a new one. Also, they came to the conclusion that most Jio customers were happy with the service, and only a small number of people complained about how slow Jio was at responding to customer service requests.

Jasrotia, Sharma, and Mishra (2019) have come up with a total of seven factors that can be used to measure how customers react to Jio services. These factors are: tariffs, internet speed, brand endorsement, value-added services, goodwill of service provider, image of brand, and innovative company. The study also showed that Reliance has caused several key service providers to close or merge, and that this has changed how the telecom industry used to work. People now care more about price as well as the speed of the internet, the quality of voice calls, and so on.

Jyothika (2019) looked at how price affects the share of service providers in the telecom industry. She came to the conclusion that investors are interested in Jio shares. Existing barriers made it hard for other companies to stay in business. With the prospect of a rise in share prices, several investors have also stated that they have changed the way they invest.

Yadav, N., and Gupta, K. (2020) looked at how the launch of Reliance Jio in 2016 has changed the Indian telecom industry. In the six months since the launch, the amount of data used in India has increased by six times, to 1.2 billion GB of data per month. This makes India the country that uses the most mobile data in the world. As operator says, they were the fastest company in the world to reach 100 million subscribers in 170 days after the launch. Due to margin pressures, the Indian telecom industry, which is sensitive to price, has been consolidating. This research tries to figure out why Jio has grown so quickly, especially from an innovation point of view, and if it fits Christensen's theory of "disruptive innovation." It was found that a late entrant into the hyper-competitive telecom space shook up the sector by concentrating on process, product and service innovation, and business model innovation that shifted from voice to data. With a 4G licence for all of India, it became a provider of digital content solutions and also qualified as a disruptive innovation.

Vialle, P., et al. (2020) concluded that two companies, Free Mobile in France & Reliance Jio in India, to learn more about disruption in regulated industries. By looking at how the drivers of disruption and the strategies of disruptors work together, they were able to show that both internal and external factors may play a big role in describing the level and type of disruption. It also showed that the standard theory of disruption doesn't fully explain disruptions in regulated industries like telecommunications.

Madhavan, P. M., & Chirputkar, A. (2020) In their research, they found that even though the pandemic had stopped the world, it can't discourage Reliance Jio from becoming debt-free, through an iconic series of investments from giants all over the world. It could do all of this in just 58 days. In other words, it wants to use the present situation and the future prospects to its advantage by being the leader of digital revolution in India. It made special data plans for people who work from home that give them access to more data. With the help of WhatsApp and the money from Facebook, the company is in negotiations with the world's biggest tech company about launching an online grocery shopping platform. Reliance Jio's long-term goal has always been to turn Indian homes into digital homes by making home automation possible. Jio wants to make devices that are as good as Apple TV set-top boxes and Amazon's Alexa, which are used all over the world. Reports from Reuters say that the specifications of Jio's digital devices are similar to those of tech giants like Apple and Amazon. But what makes Jio stand out is that they offer these features at much lower prices than the others. This helps them stay in business and become the biggest player on the Indian market (PJAEE, 17(6), 2020:4460). For example, an Apple TV 4K costs between Rs. 15,500 and Rs. 17,500, while Jio's set-top box comes with their internet service and only costs Rs. 8,200 per year. This makes it easier for people in India to use Jio. Since Jio was the first company in India to use VoLTE, it is likely that it will also be the first company in India to offer 5G. The fact that Silver Lake Partners reinvested in Reliance Jio shows that many companies around the world want to get a piece of this company, which is doing well and looking to the future. It wants to keep being the biggest telecom operator in India, and it also wants to expand its services into other digital area.

Gautam, S., Agarwal, A., (2022) mentioned that Reliance Jio uses different business models to help figure out how to make more money. The business model of Reliance helps to figure out what services the company offers and who its customers are. Reliance JIO uses a model called "loss-leading," which means that it sells products at lower prices than its competitors in order to get more customers. Jio changed its pricing strategy at the beginning and offered its services to customers at a lower rate than BSNL. This lets the company give the best deals to its customers. Reliance Jio makes money in another way by selling wireless services to its clients.

RESEARCH GAP

The term disruptive innovation is an unexplored and untapped area in the Indian context. The series of inventions and innovations which have disrupted the market place existing players and the amount of business losses suffered by them has not been captured comprehensively by any previous researchers. The literature in the Indian context on disruptive innovation is rare and seldom. The authors Jayant Bhattacharya in his book 'Disruptive Innovation- Strategies for the Enterprise Growth' and P.G. Dastur, Sandeep Sawant & Baljit Bawa in their book 'Disruptive Innovation- what every business leader should know' have beautifully chaptered the various aspects of disruptive innovations in context of its understanding and business implications. The huge literature gap is found on disruptive innovations especially in Telecom sector domain.

The review has helped to find new factors, such as market share, business losses and values of Jio's competitors. When it comes to customers, the new variables are low cost, affordability, usability, customer intimacy & awareness, consumption pattern, customers' satisfaction, value of products, and demographic profile of users. The new variables for the existing literature are the amount and quality of value creation by disruptor telecom brands.

As it has been expanded earlier the concept disruptive innovation is quite unexplored area. Therefore, a huge research gap exists on the topic. It can be studied form multiple perspectives like strategies of the Reliance Jio, various factors in context of market players and consumer, disruption impact on competitors, values & benefits offered during and after disruption at last its impact on the economy, culture, policy makers, marketers and on the academicians.

03

DISRUPTIVE INNOVATION: OPPORTUNITIES, ISSUES & CHALLENGES

New technologies or ways of doing business can have a big impact on how industries work. Most people are aware of how "sharing services" on the internet are changing the taxi and hotel industries, but there are many more examples in the areas like finance, retail electricity, and cars.

These disruptive innovations can bring important benefits to consumers and competition in the form of innovative and improved services. They can also encourage established providers to come up with new ideas and compete on price. But they can also raise legitimate public policy concerns (like safety and privacy) and lead to calls for rules to control them. Established providers often try to get new providers to follow the rules that already apply to them so that they don't have as much of a competitive edge.

In June 2015, the OECD brought together experts to talk about how disruptive innovations are causing problems now and where future work could be done. Participants talked about the economic aspects of industries where these new ideas have come up, how incumbents and regulators have responded, and how competition authorities could step in, with an emphasis on competition advocacy.

In 2020, the lockdown caused by the pandemic had an effect on the telecom industry by making more mobile data, voice traffic, and residential broadband. The telecom companies did many things to improve their customers' experiences and keep making money. But many people who know about technology think that a bunch of disruptive technologies will change the telecom industry in 2021. Many of the trends in the telecom industry that were already in place were made obsolete by disruptive technologies, which led to the rise of new telecom trends. Few of the trends observed in the industry are as follows:

Disruptive Innovation- Opportunities

1. **Creation of new markets:** Disruptive innovation normally leads to making new markets. Ideas flow into the creation of innovative products and services, which disrupt the market share of existing goods and services and creates new markets. As mobile phones got better, they took business away from coin-operated cameras and digital cameras. This was because coin-operated cameras already had the same level of clarity as digital cameras. In the same way, the rise of cell phones could be blamed for the decline in sales of music players and radios in specific. The marketplace for digital cams is clearly shrinking, while the market for mobile phones is growing. The floppy disc and the CD have also vanished from the market, and the USB drives have taken their place. Creating new markets usually takes a long time because it takes time for the market for established products to shrink. But once customers are happy with new products and services, it doesn't take long to spread the word, which starts a chain reaction of people using new products and services.

2. **Cost Reduction:** Coming up with ideas and turning them into new goods and services can take a long time and cost a lot of money. But the accessibility of technology and a wide range of web-based services can make new products and services much cheaper. Several large-scale environmental factors also put pressure on companies to make products that are good for

the environment and don't cost too much. At first, disruptive innovations might seem a little expensive, but in the long run, they save money because of economies of scale and the learning curve. Even though the new generation of electric cars is expensive, they will become less expensive as investigators come up with good ways to cut costs. There are many examples of how frugal technology has been used to lower the cost of a process and, in the end, create a new class of goods or services. Small sachets of shampoo, detergent, and soap have helped companies that make fast-moving consumer goods get a bigger share of the market. This cheap innovation has helped companies break into smaller and more remote markets, building brand awareness in the process. The widespread availability of generic medicines could be seen as a breakthrough substitute to branded medicines, and the cost of medicines for patients has gone down a lot, especially when they are used for prevention.

3. **Value addition:** Value addition usually comes in the form of an extra feature that is added to a product or service before it is sold or used by the final customer. Disruptive innovations have some value because they lead to a completely different way to meet customer needs. Artificial sweeteners with no or few calories have been highly successful at giving customers what they want. Artificial sweeteners with low or no calories have been made because people are becoming more aware of living a healthy life. This is a good thing for people who are interested in health. Several industries that make drinks and foods use these sugar substitutes. When disruptive innovations work, they add value because they either lower the cost of making the product or add new features or meet other customer needs. For example, hybrid cars can be powered by either gasoline or electricity. Electric scooters from the new generation are also good examples of value-based products because they don't pollute and don't need to be fixed.

4. **Reduced complexities:** Researchers are always looking for ways to make problems less complicated. This can lead to products or services with more than one feature that can meet customers' needs. The market for smart phones with apps has reached its limit, and scholars have come up with innovative smart processes and apps that are not only faster but also less complicated. In short, customers get a lot of different apps under one roof. The applications used by the banking and insurance systems have been updated at a lightning-fast rate, which is good for the end user. Single-window services have also been set up in a number of areas, making things less complicated overall.

5. **Innovation in routine activities:** One of the most important things about disruptive technology is that it can give consumers new and noticeable benefits. When this kind of technology comes onto the market, it changes the whole business. By using disruptive technology, both people and businesses can take advantage of the benefits it brings to their daily lives.

6. **Enhances and modifies techniques:** If you want to solve the problems of your customers, you need to use modern methods. Disruptive innovation changes how a company looks at its mechanisms and how to adapt to them. It also helps the company provide better services and changes the industry as a whole.

7. **Growth of start-up businesses:** Disruptive Innovation gives start-up companies chances to get a big foothold in industries that already exist. This gives small companies just starting out a unique chance to grow quickly and possibly do better than bigger, more established companies.

8. **Business Growth and Expansion:** When an well-established business willing to embraces disruptive technology, it has great chances to grow in its current industry or in a new industry that the technology creates. This makes the economy

of the country grow as well. Companies that can smoothly add disruptive technology to the products and services they already offer can help their current customers switch to employing the disruptive technology while also bringing in new customers as they enter a new market.

9. **Utilizing India's IT Power:** India's software industry is well-established, and so as part of "Digital India," plans are well under way to improve connectivity. This would make it possible to build facilities for additive manufacturing in small towns and encourage industrial growth outside of big cities.

10. **Video streaming:** It is an evident example of how important it is to think about how disruptive technologies might change things. These days, most of the people have a video provider so that they can watch movies and TV shows. But it wasn't like this 20 years ago. When it came to video broadcasting, Cable TV & Blockbuster used to be the best. The second didn't take advantage of the chance to use the new technology that would eventually replace it.

    Netflix

    Netflix, which is the biggest online video streaming service in the world, attempted to do business with Blockbuster but couldn't. and now the Blockbuster ceased to exist and Netflix has grown to have more than 200 million subscribers now.

11. Digital transportation services started in 2014 and have been getting increasingly popular ever since. They began as a substitute to the taxis because they were more flexible and had better prices.

    Uber

    Uber, which was one of the first digital transportation services, is almost all over the world and is now one of the best examples of a disruptive technologies. This new business model makes it easy, cheap, and effective for drivers to connect with people who need transportation.

12. **Virtual reality:** Virtual reality is usually used for games and entertainment, but it can also be used to break new ground in a wide range of fields. Some businesses that can benefit from this digital disruption are interior designers, retail chains, and car manufacturers.

Samsung

One good example is Samsung, which made the Gear VR for its Galaxy phones using technology from Oculus. This technology was a massive hit, and because it was so cheap, it sold out on Amazon in just two days during the holiday season.

13. **Online Lodging:** The market for online lodging has changed, and now travellers who don't want to stay in traditional hotels have other options. So, platforms act as middlemen between people who are offering temporary housing and people who want to buy it.

Airbnb

Airbnb is the leader in this type of business. It lets anyone rent out their property and even their own residential areas. This market isn't just for low-cost rentals; it has grown to include high-end properties all over the world.

14. **Music streaming:** Just like video streaming services like Netflix took over the market, so did music streaming services. These companies give their listeners access to a huge collection of all kinds of music, and they are becoming more and more popular with people who buy digital music.

Spotify

Spotify is an online service that lets you listen to music, watch videos, and even listen to podcasts. You can find thousands of songs and audio recordings from all over the world on the platform. It's also a great way to give new artists a boost.

15. **Inter Platform instant messaging apps:** Instant messages are a disruptive technology that has changed the way people talk to each other. In the past, people used the phone and email the most to talk to each other. Now, instant messaging is now the most popular way to communicate.

WhatsApp

WhatsApp, for example, is a cross-platform instant messaging app that lets people talk to each other or a group through text messages, voice calls, or even video calls. Because it can do so many things, users prefer to start communicating with this app more than any other.

16. **Online Encyclopaedia:** It makes finding information much easier and faster. Its search engines help people find what they need quickly and accurately. It has a lot more information than the encyclopaedias that were around before.

Wikipedia

Wikipedia is by far the best online encyclopaedia. It is kept up by a group of people working together. It covers a wide range of topics and has a lot of information on more than 1.5 million pages.

17. **Augmented reality:** is another technology that is changing the way things are done and is very useful in many different fields. This technology adds virtual parts to a real world that already exists.

Pokémon Go

Augmented reality is used in games like Pokémon Go. The game uses the GPS on the phone to show the player different Pokémon that can be caught in the area where the player is.

18. **Cryptocurrency** gave economics, a field with a long history, a new direction. There are various technologies behind cryptocurrency, such as the blockchain, that make sure these currencies work and are reliable.

    Bitcoin

    Bitcoin is the most valuable currency available. Its payment system is not run by a central bank, and it is not confined to a specific server. Bitcoin's value has gone up a lot in a short amount of time, making it a very wanted item.

19. **Collaborative Commerce:** It is also called "c-commerce," is a type of e-commerce that helps buyers and sellers do business. This new way of running a business is getting bigger and pushing the limits.

    Amazon

    Amazon grew and made it easier for people to do business together. A lot of its sales come from this market, where these products are sold by independent sellers who get them to customers. Because of this, this platform acts as a market, or in other words, like a middleman.

20. **3D printing:** By digitising objects in a 3D (three-dimensional shape), 3D printers can make all kinds of things.

    Icon

    Icon is a company that uses 3D printing to make homes. Only 24 hours are needed to build a house, and they cost around $10,000.

21. **Online Education:** It is also called e-learning, was at its peak at the time of the COVID-19 pandemic. Millions of students all over the world have kept going with their education online.

Udemy

Before the pandemic, this platform was already there. But now that online education has been shown to work, it has grown into something bigger.

22. **Fast Internet Café:** Cybercafés or internet cafes are the most profitable retail businesses in the telecommunications sector, from city areas to metros, from students to anyone looking for any kind of internet service. The idea for the business is to offer modern and fast internet services on the desktop, along with services like printing, Xerox, and so on. This is wildly popular among students, people in their teens, and even adults.

23. **Cable TV Networking:** This is one of the most common telecommunications businesses that offer cable TV systems & high-speed internet access can make a lot of money. Now, people who use cable networks for everything from TV to the Internet can be charged rent every month. People also like the idea that high-demand internet connections from cable operators cost less than those from other internet service providers. This combination of services gives Reliance Jio a chance to offer its Jio Fiber as well as Set-Top Box connections in the future.

24. **Recruitment Agency for Call Centre:** The telecom and IT industries are mostly interdependent. The BPO industry is mostly made up of call centres, which are known to be a very successful business in India. Call centres are centralised facilities that handle a large number of phone calls for an organisation. There are different kinds of call centres, such as inbound call centres, outbound call centres, and customer service centres, which need different kinds of candidates who meet different criteria.

25. **Using a cell phone used to be a luxury**, but now it's a necessity. Since Reliance Jio came out, more people in India have access to cell phones than ever before, and they need to

be charged. Mobile phones used to be a luxury, but now mobile phone and internet users can't live without them.

26. **Selling Network Equipment and Devices:** The most widely used network equipment and devices include routers, adapters and access points, ethernet switches, wireless extenders, cloud storage, modem, firewalls, network adapters, and cables etc. A retail store is a good place to start selling network devices and equipment.

27. **Selling and fixing smartphones:** Smartphones are a part of everyone's daily life and business. India has a wide range of age groups and demographics, so this business has a market all over the country. It is, in fact, one of the most profitable businesses in the telecommunications industry, and it will continue to be as long as the number of "connected things" keeps growing and the use of mobile and "smart" devices keeps growing, which will shape and define the IoT space in the end.

28. **SMS Marketing:** Even though we live in the age of digital marketing even though SMS marketing is still a good way to reach people based on where they are. This is also called "mobile advertising," and it has a lot of room to grow. It is used by many brands in places like banks, e-commerce sites, and food delivery services. Bulk SMS marketing is a very useful tool for getting the word out about new products, offering discounts, and building a brand.

29. **OpenRAN Architecture:** " Open Radio Access Network (OpenRAN) architecture" is different from the traditional radio access network (RAN) architecture in that it lets network operators design and implement 4G and 5G networks by combining software and hardware components from different vendors. Leading telecom companies started using new-generation technology in 2020 to speed up network growth and cut costs.

OpenRAN gives telecom operators the chance to buy software and hardware parts from a wide range of equipment vendors.

30. **5G Networks:** Telecom companies are preparing to build 5G networks and gradually begin offering 5G services.5G will change how people use networks by giving them superfast speed and extreme low latency. At the same time, 5G will help the Internet of Things (IoT) by making it easier for a lot of machines to talk to each other. Telecom companies all over the world have already started coming up with new and different ways to use 5G.

31. **Artificial Intelligence (AI) and Machine Learning (ML):** 5G will enable the integration of AI and ML at the network edge. Both AI and ML will be used in the next generation of wireless networks to predict end-user distribution, anticipate peak traffic, and improve network capabilities. With the help of ML algorithms, telecom companies will find it easier to improve their services. Tools like chatbots and virtual assistants that are powered by AI can be used to make sure that customer service runs smoothly. Based on a customer's past, these tools make it easier to offer personalised services that keep them interested. AI/ML also makes it possible to improve the quality of the network through predictive maintenance & smart impact analysis.

32. **Computing at the mobile edge:** To keep up with the rapid rise of smartphones and IoT devices, several telecommunication companies have already begun projects to use mobile edge computing. Many people who study technology think that mobile edge computing, which is a disruptive technology, will change the telecom industry. The telecom companies would use edge computing to store and process data closer to the devices of the end users. Edge computing will also speed up the way real-time data collected and sent by connected devices is processed.

33. **The Next-Generation Internet of Things (IoT):** The COVID-19 pandemic caused businesses in many different fields to invest in IoT. Also, in 2020, there was a big rise in the demand for smart home devices. 5G's very high speed and very low latency will help the Internet of Things (IoT) by making it possible for connected devices to share real-time data almost instantly. After a pandemic, there will be a steady rise in the need for IoT devices and applications at home and in the workplace. The telecom companies need to improve and expand their networks to meet the information needs of businesses that use the latest IoT solutions and applications.

34. **Network Footprint Expansion:** Many businesses and organisations will let their employees work from home during a pandemic. In the same way, many students prefer e-Learning or live online classes to traditional classrooms. Also, 5G is expected to increase the amount of data used on mobile devices by 400% in the coming years. The telecommunications companies will expand their network footprints to meet the huge demand from businesses and home users alike.

35. **Diversified Ecosystem:** In 2020, the Open RAN Policy Coalition was made up of the biggest network operators, device makers, and chip makers. Their goal was to keep wireless technologies like 5G open and able to work with each other. The coalition members have already started projects and made plans to make it easier to design and build modular telecom networks which don't rely on just one vendor. In 2021, more telecom companies are likely to get back together, join these alliances, and make new ones to accept disruptive technologies.

Disruptive innovation- Issues

1. **Impatient Leadership:** All kinds of innovation take time. In many ways, it›s an investment that will pay off in the long

run. But if a company›s leaders are too focused on making money quickly, some of the very important innovations can be overlooked or thrown out quickly. When we think about how close the cheapest and fastest innovations are to the existing product or solution, the problems get worse. And the more similar they are to what is already being done, the less impact they have, the faster they become old, and the less they deserve to be called «innovations.» Over time, going from one small innovation to the next can feel like an organisation is just trying to keep up with the times. At the same time, competitors who invest in essential, strategic innovations that pay off much subsequently are often able to reap the benefits of the bigger opportunities.

2. **Lack of an Innovation Culture:** One of the biggest problems with innovation and creativity can be a management model that is too rigid and stuck in the past. After all, it doesn't matter if the company is open to and willing to invest in new ideas if most of the organisation can't make those ideas happen.

   Innovation is often seen as something that takes money or other resources away from profit generation. So, time is used to get the current task done as much as possible, leaving no room for innovative ideas or creative problem-solving. Since management is based on existing performance, the future will always be pushed back.

   Worse yet, these important skills aren't always taught at all. Fresh ideas are a key part of coming up with new solutions, but many companies won't spend money on training or development. Even the most highly skilled engineer can't make products that change the market overnight. Companies need to put money into creating a culture that encourages and uses these important skills.

3. **A Fear of Change:** To be innovative, one has to do something new. Established companies that have a long history often have

strong internal resistance to this. When this happens, most new ideas come from the edges of the business, from parts that aren't tied to the core model. So, they are free to be creative and explore new areas, but their ideas aren't valued by the rest of the company and are often brushed off as crazy or extreme.

This is where people often start to fear the new and different. When the company sticks to how things are usually done, no matter how different the idea is or, as we talked about earlier, how far away the proposed investments are from the current model, innovative teams can find themselves without support and internal funding.

4. **Lack of Ownership:** The hardest things for any business to do when it comes to innovation is to figure out who is responsible. Without a sense of ownership or responsibility, there is no drive to succeed. Here, though, we often have to deal with the two sides of the business innovation problem: innovation can't just be done by one department, but it still needs to be owned by someone.

   IT and digital technologies are making CTOs and CIOs more important, and organisations need people to own the idea of innovation in the same way. This is especially important when it comes to innovation. An owner needs to stand up for long-term investments or ideas that haven't been tested yet, even though the usual focus is on short-term profits and growth.

   The best way to deal with this is to create a dedicated position. This person should be part of the management team and work higher up in the structure. They should be able to reach all departments and make sure they are set up correctly (in turn, growing the previously mentioned innovation culture). But businesses with leaders who aren't patient and are afraid of change aren't likely to hire people for these kinds of roles, since the job itself would be too new.

5. **End-to-end processes:** Coming up with an idea is just the beginning of the innovation process. Once these ideas are set, they need to go through many stages of development, testing, and improvement. All ideas are required to be checked out, but not all of them will work out. People often see this as a big waste of time and money that doesn't guarantee success. And, as we already said, the emphasis on profits and short-term goals means that strategies with a higher return on investment (ROI) will often come first.

   Yet a great idea that lies undeveloped has no market potential. In the same way, skilled teams can't build on innovative ideas if they haven't developed. In this area, innovation is a form of research and development in many ways. Businesses need to be willing to give the resources and time to ensure it occurs, without implementing gates which rely too rigidly on proven market results, being ready to accept the fact that the new product and solution may never attain the global audience.

6. **Inadequate Benchmarking:** When companies focus on the present and past, there are a lot of things to compare them to. They can, for example, try to beat the KPIs they set for this year, or they can look at their competitors to see how they did. All of these will help the organisation stay competitive, and yet innovation is much more focused on the future, and these benchmarks will kill projects before they have a chance to succeed.

   Revenue and sales metrics are often one of the biggest innovation challenges in business when it comes to coming up with new ideas. Before the operation even starts, every idea is tested to see if it will work in the market. More so, a culture of chasing KPIs across an organisation can stop teams from even coming up with ideas. Solutions that don't have immediate value for KPIs will be ignored or not shared with their communities.

Before companies can ascertain its value, each idea must always be weighed against the problems it's attempting to solve. Unique ideas requires unique variables.

Obviously, these factors need to be agreed on; it's easy to chase vanity metrics even in innovation. This is why a wider process of testing and development (see the last point) and a person in charge of innovation (who can make sure these ideas are tested and judged fairly within the firm) are so important.

7. **No innovation ecosystem:** Ultimately, innovation is about coming up with new ideas. Many of these ideas come about when people from different teams share their ideas and knowledge with each other. So, a culture of silos is a huge problem for business innovation. After all, if people in a company can't work together, they can't share new ideas.

   When each team is on its own, or worse, when they are forced to compete with each other, they will focus on many of the problems listed above: chasing their own KPIs, making sure they do well so they look good to the board, and not bringing anything significantly controversial, new, or risky to the table.

   This is also why young companies and start-ups like hackathons & special ideation sessions. Organizational isolation is a major problem when it comes to creativity and innovation. An eco-system makes sure that every part of the business has a job to do. So, each department works to get funding and move forward with new solutions and ideas that can really make a difference in the world.

8. **Ongoing General Issues:** Developing nations like India are already in a tough spot because they have low human capital, weak institutions, and a hard business environment.

9. **Trust and Ethical Issues:** Disruptive technology in and of itself is not the problem. However, privacy, ownership, and

transparency are all ethical issues that can arise because of these technologies.

10. **Problems with adaptability:** Disruptive innovations take little time to prove themselves in the complex market conditions, and they also take a long time to get into the market. Disruptive innovations must also be able to change with the market.

11. **Untested & Time-Consuming:** In its early stages, new technology is usually not tried out or perfected, and its development can take years. Any new idea needs time to develop, depending on how useful it is and how well it meets market needs. It takes a long time for a new idea, product, or service to become well-known in the market.

12. **Outdated technology that is still used a lot:** New ideas or business models tend to shake up existing ideas, products, services, or business models, which makes the market very competitive. This makes it hard for new ideas to get a foothold in the market because the businesses that are already there can do anything to keep from being pushed away from the market.

13. **Problems with Network Coverage and Internet Speed:** As more people joined Jio's network after September 5, the speed of Jio's 4G data services slowed down a lot. Now, the internet data speed is between 6 and 10 Mbps, down from 50 Mbps when it first started. On record, the difference is huge, but for most customers, even an 8Mbps speed should work fine. But the Jio connection is often unstable, which makes it hard for people to use. Users have also said that speeds change even though they are in the same place.

14. **Buggy Jio apps:** Reliance Jio apps haven't always worked well, but the idea of free content goes over well with Indian people. The Jio TV app often crashes and takes a long time to start up, which is also true of most of Jio's other apps. From what

we've seen, the Jio4GVoice app is one of the most buggy ones. The app doesn't load very often, and when it does, it's pretty slow.

15. **Older phones don't support VOLTE:** People who don't have phones that support VOLTE can't even make voice calls without using the Jio4GVoice app, which, as we've already said, seems to have bugs. Because of this one problem, most new customers won't use the feature that lets them make free voice calls. Most of Indian smartphone or mobile users are still stuck with 3G phones, but they can use VOLTE. They won't get anything out of the Jio Sims.

16. **Battery Consumption:** Reliance Jio's internet services are now available on the 4G band. Since there isn't much of a price difference between 2G, 3G, and 4G, more and more people are choosing Jio. The only problem with 4G services is that they drain the phone's battery, which means the user has to charge the phone more often. If there are no 2G or 3G options, the consumer can't save battery life by switching to a slower connection.

Disruptive Innovation- Challenges

1. **Adaptability:** Disruptive innovations take little time to prove itself in complex market conditions, and they also take a long time to penetrate the market. Disruptive innovations must also be able to change with the market. Established market players may create distractions to make a new product, process, or service less stable or show that it doesn't work. In the 2000s, dishwashers were introduced to the Indian market, but they didn't work well there because maids run most Indian kitchens and homes. This new product didn't do well on the market, but the companies also didn't do enough to market it.

2. **Gestation Period:** It takes a long time for a new idea, product, or service to gain market traction. There are certain taboos in the culture of the market, which makes it take longer for an innovation to come along and change the market. Electric scooters have been around in India for about four or five years, but they still can't catch on. Any new idea needs time to develop, depending on how useful it is and how well it meets market needs. It also depends on how well the manufacturer can make it and if it meets the needs of the customer. Any new product or service has to break into the market, which depends on how well the idea spreads through the market, which in turn determines how long it takes for the product to be born.

3. **Increased competition:** Creative ideas or business models have a tendency to shake up ideas, products, services, or business models that have been around for a long time. This makes the market very competitive. This makes it hard for new ideas to get off the ground because established businesses will do anything to keep from going out of business. The established companies might even lobby for the new companies to follow the rules that are already in place, so that the new companies have less of an effect on them and the established companies have a competitive edge. In India, traditional rickshaws and taxis are competing with online hotel searches as well as taxi sharing services. In the same way, online food delivery apps have also changed the way individuals look for food. Because there is more competition, there may be good reasons to worry about public policy and may be a need for regulation.

4. **Market Acceptance:** It takes a long time for a new idea to get a significant share of the market. This is because established companies in the market are resistant and compete with new ones, and because it takes time for the market to accept a new business model, product, or service. Customers now shop in a different way than they did before the internet. Customers are

starting to want to buy things online instead of in stores. But this didn't happen all at once. Online stores like Amazon, Flipkart, and Myntra have worked to educate their customers and make the market aware of how easy and safe it is to shop online. Items that cost a lakh rupees or more can now be bought online. Customers no longer have to leave their homes to buy a pair of shoes or a piece of clothing. Customers today know how to use the internet and prefer to buy these products online because it's easy to shop, it's easy to return items, and there's a guarantee.

5. **Longer-Term Sustainability is a Concern:** Having said that, it should also be noted that Reliance is putting a lot of money into its venture and has already spent close to $2 billion on it. It is also taking the risk of "disruption with discounts," which might not work in the long run. In fact, its plan is to get as many subscribers as possible so that the higher volumes can make up for the razor-thin margins. Its strategy has worked, as can be seen by the fact that it has gained close to 200 million new subscribers. But it's still not clear if these customers will stick with it once the initial excitement caused by freebies and subsidies wears off and the subsidies end.

6. **Changing Government Policies:** While discussing about bandwidth, Indian telecom sector has to deal with the additional challenge of having to bid for highly priced spectrum, which is sometimes "tainted" by accusations of corruption and crony capitalism. In fact, this problem is so common in India that several world's biggest telecom companies are often hesitant to enter the marketplace.

In addition to this, they are also put off by the fact that government rules and regulations are always changing. For example, tax laws that govern mergers and acquisitions are sometimes changed "retroactively."

7. **Compliance and Legal Violations:** Customers and regulators hope companies will find risks to the privacy and security of customer data in the cloud, deal with them, and reduce them. Consumers want companies to be clear about where their information goes, who sees it and what it will be used for.

8. **Data Breaches:** Even with the best controls, data security breaches do occur, but encryption and handling of data have proven to be helpful ways to deal with them. On the 40th day of the lockdown, it was reported that a database with information about people who used Reliance Jio's Covid-19 symptom checker was found on the internet without any security. The tool was made by Jio to help people self-test for COVID-19 based on the symptoms they were having. It was available on Jio's official website and mobile app. A database of users who had used Jio's symptom checker was found to have no security. This database had information like the user's name, where they lived, and a list of all their symptoms.

9. **User privacy:** Issues about customer privacy reached an all-time high in 2018, when many companies had high-profile data leaks that put their customers' private information at risk. Notably, it was said that Marriott International Inc. had a security breach that let 500 million customers' personal information out into the open. Through the attack, hackers were able to get customers' names, phone numbers, email addresses, passport numbers, travel information, and payment information. With more and more breaches like this, it's hard for companies to collect this data without violating their users' privacy or giving their personal information to bad people.

10. **Fairness and Equity:** Machine learning is still an interesting type of disruptive technology for many uses, because it gives people the chance to make important decisions and judgments

without their own biases getting in the way. But this will only work if both the dataset and the model are free of bias. In October 2018, for example, it was reported that Amazon had gotten rid of a machine learning tool that picked the best resumes from job applicants because it was unfair to women. The tool was likely biased because it was trained on a set of curriculum vitae from previous applicants, most of whom were men.

11. **Reputational Risk:** Microsoft's "Tay" chatbot is a cautionary tale of an AI system that went bad and caused the company a lot of trouble. Tay "learned" from the people she talked to on Twitter. Some of them "taught" her to say extreme and racist things. After only one day on the platform, the bot was shut down quickly. Even though the backlash from Tay wasn't too bad, letting AIs run unchecked can pose a major risk to your business's reputation and bottom line. It could even put your business out of business. Artificial Intelligence technology that are prone to mistakes, can be biased, or are easy to hack can make the bad goodwill of the organisation look bad in the eyes of the public, as the Australian government found out when they used an algorithm to find welfare fraud. Because of bugs in the algorithm, thousands of people on welfare got notices that they owed money when they didn't. In the end, this caused a lot of people to get angry, and the Australian Senate started an official investigation.

12. **Fake chatbots:** Scammers can make a bad chatbot that looks like a real business and put it in an app store where customers of the real business can get assistance and download the fake chatbot. From there, they have a direct line to that customer and can ask for all the sensitive and personally identifiable information (PII) they need to help the real client with their real question. To make things even more confusing, hackers might not even need people to download an app for a spoofed chatbot

to show up. With malware, they might be able to put their fake chatbot right on the real website of the company.

13. **Ethical and legal concerns:** Since AI systems get smarter and more autonomous, figuring out how to deal with their ethical and legal problems will be the most important thing. For eg, companies that study self-driving cars have to deal with their individual versions of philosophical problems like the trolley problem. If an accident is going to happen anyway, is it okay for a self-driving car to change its path to save more people, even if it puts the lives of its passengers at risk? Whose lives should be saved first: the people in the car or the people on the street?

14. **Greater Complexity in the Internet of Things (IoT):** Ericsson predicts that by 2022, 29 billion devices, including smartphones, GPS devices, "Smart" thermostats, and toasters, will be connected to the Internet of Things. This huge growth of the Internet of Things gives bad people billions of new ways to attack. Companies need to make sure that their Internet of Things (IoT) devices are safe and have no default passwords and all security updates.

15. **Public Safety:** Data hackings that expose customers' personal and financial information are bad enough, but the effects are limited to the person who was affected. What happens when attackers get into an IoT network that controls public infrastructure? There are a lot of things that could go wrong, from controlling traffic lights to shutting down power plants. When the IoT is used with infrastructure like power grids, both cyber and physical security are required to keep them safe. In 2003, there was a huge blackout in the Northeast that adversely affected more than 50 million people. This shows what could happen in the worst case during an IoT attack

04

DISRUPTIVE INNOVATION STRATEGY IN INDIAN TELECOM SECTOR

It has been around for more than 160 years. In 1851, the government set up the first working telegraph lines near Kolkata, which was then called Calcutta. However, it wasn't until 1881 that India got its first official telephone service. Communication has grown and changed since the beginning of time. The first way people talked to each other was by moving to places near rivers so they could see each other more easily. Then, people used smoke signals and drums to send messages and keep in touch. Then came written mail, Morse code, telegraphs, telex, and the telephone, which made it possible for people to talk faster and farther away. We have radio, TV, fax, e-mail, and the internet today. What differentiates presently development in communication from those of the past is the invention themselves. It's that the inventions themselves will speed up the rate of new ideas. This means that we'll need to learn always new ways to do things.

Changes in the way the industry works bring up a number of problems. Changes in customer tastes and a rise in the use of over-the-top (OTT) services to connect have hurt revenue from traditional sources like voice. Also, there has been a huge increase in data traffic, but there hasn't been a corresponding increase in revenue, and the costs of updating networks to fulfil the demand for bandwidth have gone up. As telecom companies try to deal with these problems, they need to look at four things: operational efficiency, network optimization, revenue streams, and customer experience.

India's business model changes have been led by the telecommunications industry. Business model innovation refers to the process of changing an organisation by using strategic partnerships and/or realigning an existing business strategy to reposition the business or expand into new markets. Since India's economic policies became more open, telecommunications products have changed a lot. This has led to significant, ongoing, and fast innovation. India's telecom companies have used different models. Even the same operator uses different models in different places based on what the customers want. These are the lowest tariffs in the world. The vastly improved and expanded telecommunication services have had a big impact on the economy and helped the country's GDP grow in a big way.

MAJOR INNOVATIONS IN TELECOM

The three major technological innovations that have been taken place in communication are-

- Innovations in computerization, digitalization, and miniaturisation
- Innovation to the Internet, mobile communications, and packet-based Next Generation Networks (NGN) are causing services to come together.
- Innovations related to ICT as a general technology to redesign and streamline production, administration, and transaction processes to create new products and services for the information society.

Here are some innovations in the telecom industry that have changed the way things work.

1. Internet: At the beginning of the 2000s, the Internet posed a challenge to the Telecom sector, which had been the only player in the communication market with voice mail, text messages, etc.

2. VoIP: It is an IP-based application that makes it easy for users to talk to each other. It is used to send and receive voice calls in real time.

It is a quick, easy, and cheap way for users to make VoIP calls that is bundled of P2P technology. Skype's features include video and audio chat, Skype in, Skype Voicemail, Skype SMS, and more. The tariff rates are cheaper in respect of traditional tariff and Skype to Skype and other VoIP platforms is absolutely free. It is an effective way to get a lot of people to use something.

3. Integration with providers of content service: Keeping in touch keeps getting cheaper. Connectivity is taking up less of the information value chain, while content, services, and products are taking up more. By 2020, it's likely that a content company will buy one or more of the big telecom companies.

4. The Internet of Things (IoT): The next big thing that will have an effect is the boom of devices that can talk to each other. This will connect billions of new data sources around the world by 2020. All of these devices will lead to a huge increase in the amount of data. We will quickly move past Exabytes and move to the world of Zettabytes every year.

5. Mobility: The growth of mobile connections is much faster than the growth of fixed line connections. This makes sense, since most growth is happening in poorer parts of the world and in the developing world. Even when they can use a landline, mobile is cheaper, more convenient, and more beneficial for these people.

6. Market Saturation: As the elderly population ages and retires, they will move into fully digitalized retirement communities and assisted living facilities. The world will force older people to use these technologies, and they will probably use a lot more bandwidth than they or their carriers ever thought they would. When this happens, the last remaining market penetration percentages will be reached, and the market will be fully saturated.

7. Security: Carriers play a key role in fighting new threats because they are in charge of the networks. Customers will start to expect and then demand more proactive security from all parts of the internet value chain, & carriers will have to meet these expectations with a variety of technological and operational changes.

8. New Disruptive Business Model: Reliance Jio told customers about a new and interesting business offer. The operator started a new plan on September 5, 2016. Here are some of the most important parts:

- Postpaid mode available on tariff plans above ₹499/-
- Everyone who signed up got free data and voice services until December 31, 2016;
- No roaming fees for any plan;
- You can use apps worth 15,000/- for free until December 2017;
- Extra 25% discount for students

THE HISTORICAL RECORD OF DISRUPTIONS IN THE INDIAN TELECOM SECTOR

In the past, the Indian telecom industry has always been disrupted in the same way that the global telecom sector is disrupted over and over again as new technologies come out.

In fact, less within a generation, the Global Telecom sector has evolved from providing basic mobile phones with the bare minimum of services to the start of the smartphone revolution and the release of successive generations of wireless technologies.

When the 2nd Generation of wireless technology, or 2G, came out, many people thought it would be around for just a few years before the next generation came out. But 2G quickly became 3G, which was then followed by 4G, which could be replaced by 5G in the coming years.

With all of these trends, it's hard for telecom providers to keep up with so many changes in such a short amount of time. This means that they have to constantly update their infrastructure and technologies. So, it can be said that "change is the only constant" in the Global Telecom sector. This is something that all Telecom Majors around the world have to keep in mind when making plans and putting them into action.

Also, the Global Telecom Sector is threatened by hardware that becomes outdated too quickly. Since new versions of Smartphone handsets come out every few months, it's hard for them to plan ahead and figure out how compatible and interoperable the handsets are with their infrastructure.

Changing Governmental Policies

When it comes to bandwidth, the Indian telecom industry has to deal with the extra challenge of sometimes having to bid on expensive spectrum, especially when such spectrum auctions are "tainted" by accusations of corrupt practices and crony capitalism. In fact, this problem is so common in India that many of the world's biggest telecom companies are often hesitant to enter the Indian market.

EVOLUTION OF MOBILE COMMUNICATION (1G, 2G AND 3G)

Mobile communications systems revolutionized the way people communicate. Any radio telephone capable of operating while moving at any speed, battery operated and small enough to be carried by a person comes under the mobile communication systems. Mobile telephones offer full-duplex transmission. These are one-to-one systems that permit two simultaneous transmissions. Since the commercial introduction of Advanced Mobile Phone System (AMPS) service in 1983, mobile communication systems have witnessed an explosive growth. The most important breakthrough was the cellular concept. The advent of cellular operation brought frequency reuse capabilities. Advances in wireless access, digital signal processing, integrated circuits, increased battery life, etc led to exponential growth of personal communication services. Cellular telephones began as a simple two-way analog communication system using frequency modulation for voice and frequency-shift keying for transporting control and signalling information. Other cellular systems are a **digital cellular system, cordless telephony, satellite mobile, and paging.**

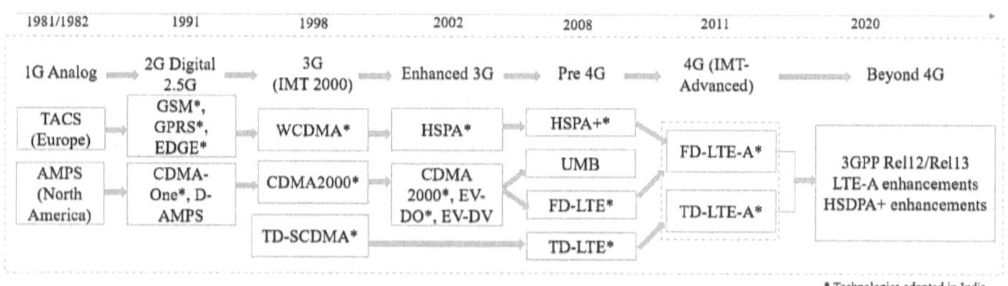

Figure 4.1

Source: *"Evolution path of Mobile Communication"*
Telecom Regulatory Authority of India

Multiple Access Schemes

Before we venture in time to look at the past, present and future of mobile technology, let's take a look at different multiple access schemes.

Requirements for a multiple access scheme

In any cellular system it is necessary for it to be able have a scheme whereby it can handle multiple users at any given time. There are many ways of doing this, and as cellular technology has advanced, different techniques have been used.

There are a number of requirements that any multiple access scheme must be able to meet:

- Ability to handle several users without mutual interference.
- Ability to be able to maximize the spectrum effciency
- Must be robust, enabling ease of handover between cells.

FDMA - Frequency Division Multiple Access

FDMA is the most straightforward of the multiple access schemes that have been used. As a subscriber comes onto the system, or swaps from one cell to the next, the network allocates a channel or frequency to each one. In this way the different subscribers are allocated a different slot and access to the network. As different frequencies are used, the system is naturally termed Frequency Division Multiple Access. This scheme was used by all analogue systems.

TDMA - Time Division Multiple Access

The second system came about with the transition to digital schemes for cellular technology. Here digital data could be split up in time and sent as bursts when required. As speech was digitised it could be sent in short data bursts, any small delay caused by sending the data in bursts would be short and not noticed. In this way it became possible to organise the system so that a given number of slots were available on a give transmission. Each subscriber would then be allocated a different time slot in which they could transmit or receive data. As different time slots are used for each subscriber to gain access to the system, it is known as time division multiple access. Obviously, this only allows a certain number of users access to the system. Beyond this another channel may be used, so systems that use TDMA may also have elements of FDMA operation as well.

CDMA - Code Division Multiple Access

The scheme has been likened to being in a room filled with people all speaking different languages. Even though the noise level is very high, it is still possible to understand someone speaking in your own language. With CDMA different spreading or chip codes are used. When generating a direct sequence spread spectrum, the data to be transmitted is multiplied with spreading or chip code. This widens the spectrum of the signal, but it can only be decided in the receiver if it is again multiplied with the same spreading code. All signals that use different spreading codes are not seen, and are discarded in the process. Thus, in the presence of a variety of signals it is possible to receive only the required one.

In this way the base station allocates different codes to different users and when it receives the signal it will use one code to receive the signal from one mobile, and another spreading code to receive the signal from a second mobile. In this way the same frequency channel can be used to serve a number of different mobiles.

1. FIRST GENERATION (ANALOG)

First-generation mobile systems used circuit switched analog transmission to carry low-quality voice traffic. In 1979, the first cellular system in the world became operational by Nippon Telephone and Telegraph (NTT) in Tokyo, Japan. In the United States, the Advanced Mobile Phone System (AMPS) was launched in 1982. The two most popular analog systems were Nordic Mobile Telephones (NMT) and Total Access Communication Systems (TACS). All the standards in 1G use frequency modulation techniques for voice signals and all the handover decisions were taken at the Base Stations. The spectrum within the cell was divided into a number of channels and every call is allotted a dedicated pair of channels.

Network Standards

The first generation of mobile communication technology consists of multiple standards such as AMPS, NMT, TACS among others.

- **AMPS:** It is based on FDMA to allow multiple user access in a cell. Cell-sizes were not fixed under this standard and an eight-mile radius was used in urban areas and a twenty-five-mile radius in rural areas. With the increase in a number of users, new cells were added and with the addition of new cells the frequency plans needed to be reworked to avoid interference related issues. There were security issues too with this and impersonation was easy if someone was able to get hold of another person's serial code.
- **NMT:** NMT was based on analog technology and was developed in two versions; NMT 450 and NMT 900. The numbers indicate the frequency bands used. This standard specified billing and roaming but its specifications lacked in security as the traffic was not encrypted. The cell sizes in an NMT network range from 2

km to 30 km. NMT used full duplex transmission, allowing for simultaneous reception and transmission of voice.

Access Technology

In the first generation of mobile telecommunication, Frequency Division Multiple Access (FDMA) technique was used which allows a number of users to share the available frequency by segmenting the frequency block into smaller subcarriers and allocating those subcarriers on a per-user basis. In FDMA, each phone call is assigned to a specific uplink frequency channel and other downlink frequency channel. The channel, therefore, is closed to other conversations until the initial call is finished, or until it is handed-off to a different channel.

2. SECOND GENERATION (2G)

Second Generation or 2G technology was introduced in the early 1990s' as the first generation of digital radio technologies. Those circuit-switched data services were developed as a replacement for analog cellular networks. Specifically, through digital systems, the voice is taken through the handset and passes from an analog to digital converter so that what comes out is a series of bits (bitstream). Additionally, Second Generation technologies introduced services such as SMS (Short Message Services) and MMS (Multimedia Message Services) which are digitally encrypted.

Network Standards

The second generation of mobile communications technologies was developed mainly on four standards, namely, Global System for Mobile Communications (GSM), Interim Standard 136 (IS-136), Code Division Multiple Access – 1 (CDMA-1) or Interim Standard 95 (IS -95), and PDC (Personal Digital Cellular).

- **GSM:** It is a standard developed by European Telecommunications Standards Institute (ETSI) designed to provide services such as voice mail, text messaging, international roaming, prepaid calling, SMS, etc. The early GSM systems used a 25MHz frequency spectrum in a 900MHz band. This spectrum is then divided into 124 carrier frequencies of 200 KHz each. A single 200 KHz channel was shared between eight users by allocating a unique time slot to each one of them. The cell radius in the GSM network varies depending upon the antenna height, antenna gains, propagation conditions, etc.

- **CDMA** One/IS-95: It is a wireless interface protocol that was standardized in 1993 which supports up to 64 users that are orthogonally coded and simultaneously transmitted on each 1.25 MHz channel. All users share the same 1,250 kHz wide carrier, but unique digital codes are used to differentiate subscribers. The codes are shared by both the mobile station and the base station and are called "pseudo-random code sequences". Base stations in the system distinguish themselves from each other by transmitting different portions of the code at a given time.

Access Technology

In the second-generation telecom systems, multiple access is achieved by TDMA and CDMA techniques.

Evolved 2G Systems

Due to a demand of high efficiency and capacity in the second-generation networks, some enhancements have been done in the existing network architecture, which came to be known as 2.5G. It provided support for packet-switched data services in addition to circuit switched data service that 2G used to support. The major enhancements in 2.5G are as follows:

- Introduction of **General Packet Radio Service (GPRS)** into the GSM specifications. GPRS provides faster data rates by aggregating several time slots into a single bearer. It takes all eight timeslots from GSM (which is a TDMA system) in a 200 kHz bandwidth giving a theoretical data rate of 8 x14.4=115kbps. In practice though, it supports up to 56kbps and up to 4 timeslots.

- **Enhanced Data Rates for Global Evolution (EDGE)** also known as Enhanced GPRS is digital mobile phone technology that allows improved data transmission rates as a backward-compatible extension of GSM. It is considered a pre-3G radio technology. It is an evolution of the GPRS radio modulation to higher data rates within the same 200 kHz bandwidth used by GSM and GPRS. It adds the capability of 8- PSK (Phase ShiG Keying) modulation to transmit 3bits per waveform (using 1 of 8 phrases) compared to the only 1bit per waveform using GMSK (Gaussian-filtered Minimum ShiG Keying) modulation as used in GSM and GPRS.

3. THIRD GENERATION (3G)

The ever-growing needs of subscribers and the several technological advances that existed in the early 2000s led the market to the development of the third-generation technology which focused on the improvement of voice services with some data capabilities. Those systems were developed with the aim of offering high-speed data and multimedia connectivity to subscribers. The International Telecommunication Union (ITU) has defined 3G systems as being capable of supporting high-speed data ranges of 144 kbps to greater than 2 Mbps.

Network Standard

The third generation of mobile technologies focused on the improvement of voice services, higher bandwidths and the support of multimedia services which are mainly developed on two technology standards: Universal Mobile Telecommunication System (UMTS) and CDMA-2000.

- **UMTS:** It is third generation successor of second– generation GSM-based cellular technologies including GPRS and EDGE, which is managed by 3GPP (Third Generation Partnership Programme). UMTS is also referred to as WCDMA as it uses Wideband CDMA (W-CDMA) to carry the radio transmissions. It employs a 5 MHz channel bandwidth. Using this bandwidth, it has the capacity to carry over 100 simultaneous voice calls, or it can carry data at speeds up to 2 Mbps in its original format. In FDD, the transmission and reception of signals are achieved simultaneously using two different frequencies. For the FDD scheme to operate satisfactorily there is a guard band between transmission and reception frequencies to enable the receiver not to be unduly affected by the transmitter signal.

TDD uses only a single frequency for full duplex transmission control that shares the channel between transmission and reception, spacing them apart by multiplexing the two signals on a time basis. It is used with data transmissions (data or digitized voice), transmitting a short burst of data in each direction. As the transmission periods are relatively short no time delay is noticed on voice transmissions resulting from the time delays introduced by using TDD.

- **CDMA-2000:** It is a third-generation (3G) standard developed by the

  International Telecommunication Union (ITU). Data communication speeds ranging from 114 Kbps to 2 Mbps are supported by this standard.CDMA-2000 denotes a family of standards that represent the successive revolutionary stages of the underlying technology, namely, CDMA2000 1x, CDMA2000 1x EV-DO (Evolution Data Optimized), and CDMA2000 1x EV-DV (Evolution Data and Voice).

  CDMA2000 1X which is also standardized as IS-2000 supports circuit-switched voice and has the capability to provide up to and sometimes beyond 35 simultaneous calls per sector and as such it doubles the capacity of the original IS-95 networks. It also enables the transmission and reception of data at rates up to 153 kbps in both directions.

  CDMA2000 1x EV-DO only carries data, but at speeds up to 3.1Mbps in the forward direction and 1.8 Mbps in the reverse direction, the speed in the reverse link being upgraded as part of Release A of the standard

Evolved 3G Systems

Due to the convergence of Internet and Wireless Communications, a tremendous growth has been observed in mobile network services. Also, 3G Systems had some limitations related to coverage and access speed, power consumption, the complexity of the system, etc. This led the industry to find ways to update the already existing air interface standards and replace them with improved versions. This was done with the deployment of the updated versions of W-CDMA and CDMA 2000, High-Speed Packet Access (HSPA) and 1xEV-DO.

HSPA (also known as 3.5G) is the evolved version of W-CDMA which consists of two individual technology standards, i.e., High-Speed Downlink Packet Access (HSDPA) and High-Speed Uplink Packet Access (HSUPA).

- **HSDPA:** It is an upgrade to the original 3G UMTS cellular system that provides much greater download speeds for data. Using HSDPA, peak user data rates of 10 Mbps within the 5 MHz channel bandwidth offered under 3G UMTS can be achieved. It improves the overall network packet data capacity, improves the spectral efficiency and enables networks to achieve a lower delivery cost per bit along with higher data speeds as well as shorter service response times and better availability of services to users.
- **HSUPA:** HSUPA is the companion technology to HSDPA, applied to the uplink from the User Equipment (UE) to the NodeB or base station and provides a considerable increase in speed for users in the uplink. It allows peak uplink raw data rates of 5.74 Mbps. To facilitate the improved performance, the Hybrid ARQ (Automatic Repeat reQuest) used for HSDPA is also employed for the uplink, HSUPA. To reduce latency, fast packet scheduling has been adopted for the uplink as for the downlink with a slightly different variation.

Table 4.1: Comparative Chart for Mobile Communication Generation

Technology	1G	2G/2.5G	3G
Start / development	1970/1984	1980/1999	2000/2010
Data Bandwidth	2 Kbps	14.4-64 Kbps	2 Mbps
Standards	AMPS	2G: TDMA, CDMS, GSM 2.5: GPRS, EDGE	WCDMA, CDMA – 2000
Technology	Analog Cellular Technology	Digital Cellular Technology	Broad bandwidth CDMA, IP technology
Service	Mobile Telephony (Voice)	2G; Digital Voice, SMS 2.5G: Higher capacity packetized data	Integrated Higher Quality audio, video and data
Multiplexing	FDMA	TDMA, CDMA	CDMA
Switching	Circuit	2G; Circuit 2.5G: Circuit for access network and air interface: packet for core network and data	Packet except circuit for air interface
Core Network	PSTN	PSTN	Packet network
Note	During 1G wireless phones were used for voice only.	2g allowed multiple users to use a single channel via multiplexing. In 2.5G multimedia services and streaming grew. Phones started supporting web browsers.	3G had multimedia services support along with streaming. Universal access and portability across different device types was made possible.

EVOLUTION OF MOBILE COMMUNICATIONS (4G AND 5G)

Mankind was getting services, opportunities, entertainment, education and much more at the click of a button or touch of the screen. As a result demand expanded and so did the mobile consumers. In the field of automation, Internet of Things (IoT) also started gaining limelight. With connectivity and IoT technologies it became possible for a doctor to perform surgery sitting miles away, through a robot, by using internet. Hence the need for faster speed and better connectivity aroused. To meet these needs fourth generation of mobile technology was introduced in 2010. With the entry of new operator(s) in the mobile services using 4G technology, these services expanded quickly particularly in India. Now focus is shifted to 5G (Fifth Generation) technologies. Operators in countries like South Korea, Japan and China are making efforts to start 5G commercial services soon.

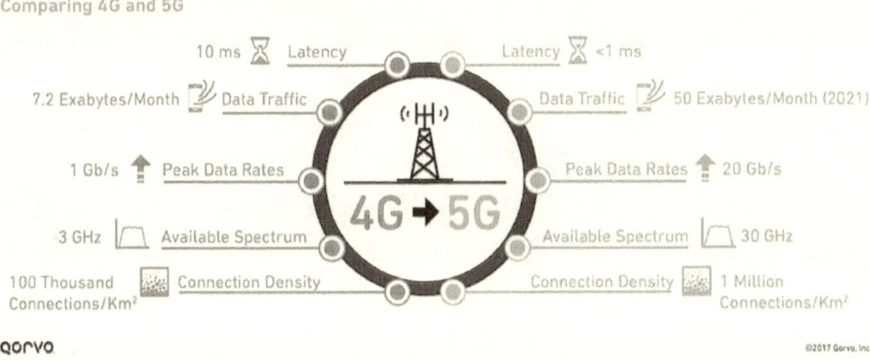

Transition from 4G to 5G (Src – Qorvo)

Figure 4.2

Source: *Qorvo (2015) is an American semiconductor company that designs, manufactures, and supplies radio-frequency systems and solutions for applications that drive wireless and broadband communications, as well as foundry services*

4. FOURTH GENERATION (4G)

Fourth Generation (4G) of broadband cellular network technology is based on the capabilities defined by the ITU (International Telecommunication

Union) in IMT Advanced (International Mobile Telecommunications Advanced) which supersede the 3G. It is popularly referred to as MAGIC which is the acronym for "Mobile multimedia, Any-where, Global mobility solutions over, Integrated wireless and Customized services". According to the ITU, a 4G network requires a mobile device to be able to exchange data at 100 Mbps for high mobility communication and 1 Gbps for low mobility communication.

Network Standards

There are multiple 4G mobile technology standards used by different cellular providers that conform to 4G requirements, namely, LTE (pre - 4G), LTE-Advanced, WiMAX, and Ultra Mobile Broadband (UMB).

LTE: The UMTS (Universal Mobile Telecommunications Service) cellular technology upgrade termed as Long-Term Evolution (LTE), which is also sometimes called 3.9G or Super 3G, is to accomplish higher speeds along with lower packet latency. A number of new technologies were introduced by LTE as compared to the previous cellular systems. For example, the OFDMA (Orthogonal Frequency Division Multiple Access) technology and the SC-FDMA (Single- Carrier FDMA) technology. The UMTS architecture that was used in 3G (Third Generation) consisted of the Radio Network Controller (RNC) controls the Node Bs and performs resource management and connects to the Serving GPRS Support Node (SGSN). In LTE both the function of NodeB and RNC is performed by ENodeB – Evolved NodeB

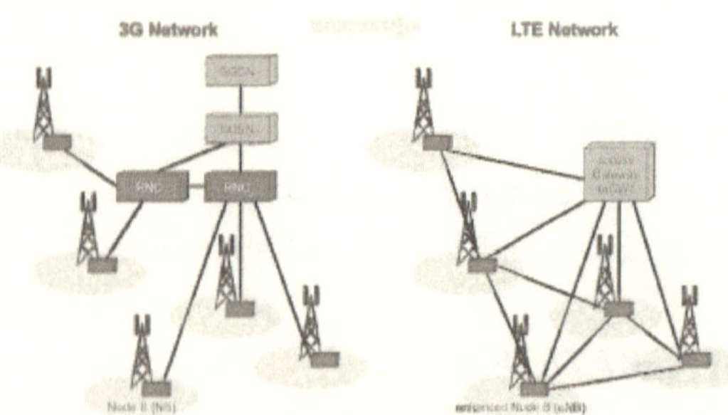

Figure 4.3: Evolution from UMTS technology used in 3G to LTE used in 4G

LTE- Advanced: For LTE Advanced / IMT Advanced, the number of key requirements and key features has been specified; some of them are as follows:

- To have maximum downlink speed of 1Gbps
- To have maximum uplink speed of 500 Mbps
- To have latency less than or equal to 10ms
- To have peak spectrum efficiency of downlink as 30bps/Hz and uplink as 15bps/Hz
- Should possess the ability to support scalable bandwidth upto 100MHz

MIMO (Multiple Input Multiple Output) and OFDM are two of the base technologies that will facilitate LTE Advanced to achieve the high data throughput rates. Along with these, there are a number of other technologies that will be employed to achieve requirements specified for LTE-advanced. These are:

Carrier Aggregation (CA): Carrier Aggregation utilises multiple channels either in the same bands or in different bands of the spectrum. This solves the problem of insufficient contiguous spectrum to provide the required bandwidths for the very high data rates.

Coordinated Multipoint: Poor performance at the cell edges remains one of the key issues with many cellular systems. The data rates reduce due to interference from adjacent cells. A solution to this problem can be joint scheduling and transmissions as well as joint processing of the received signals. For LTE-Advanced this scheme known as coordinated multipoint. In this way, a UE (User Equipment) at the edge of a cell can be served by two or more eNodeBs (LTE Base Station Component). This will allow improvement in received and transmitted signals which in turn will increase the throughput at the cell edge.

LTE Relaying: LTE relaying is a scheme that enables signals to be forwarded by remote stations from the main base station to improve coverage.

As mentioned earlier there are two access technologies used in Fourth Generation telecom

OFDMA: In Frequency Division Multiplexing, the total bandwidth is divided into several non-overlapping frequency bands. Each band is used to carry a separate signal. This way a single bandwidth can be utilised to send a number of signals without any interference amongst them. When modulation of any type - voice, data, etc. is applied to a carrier, then the sidebands spread out on either side of frequency range. For successful demodulation of the data, it is necessary for a receiver to receive the whole signal to successfully demodulate the data. This requires spacing between the transmitted signals so that they can be effectively filtered. This space is known as the guard band. But such is not the case with OFDMA (Orthogonal Frequency Division Multiple Access). Even though the sidebands from each carrier fold over each other, the signals can still be received without the expected interference because the carrier signals are orthogonal (statistically independent) to each other.

SC-FDMA: Due to the superposition of all the orthogonal signals, OFDMA has a high Peak to Average Power Ratio (PAPR). Signals with high PAPR require higher energy to be transmitted to long distances. Since base station acquires a definite land area in each circle which is big enough to provide high energy sources, therefore OFDMA is suitable for downlinks. But there is a limited battery life of each mobile and it cannot render such high-power signals to the base station for significant time period. As a result, LTE uses a modulation scheme for uplink communication known as SC-FDMA (Single Carrier FDMA), which is a hybrid format that combines the low peak to average ratio offered by single-carrier systems with the multipath interference resilient and flexible subcarrier frequency allocation that OFDMA provides.

5. FIFTH GENERATION (5G)

The forecast for future 10 years' traffic demand illustrates an increase in 1000 scales and more than 100 billion connections of Internet of Things.

This foists a big challenge for future mobile communication technology beyond year 2020. The consumers demand a high-speed data at low prices. 5G is targeted to resolve these contradictory demands towards year 2020. 5G was labelled as 'ultra-fast, ultra-reliable, ultra-high capacity transmitting at super low latency' by the National Infrastructure Commission in the report "5G Infrastructure Requirements in the UK" (2016). Facilities that might be seen with 5G technology include far better levels of connectivity and coverage. The term World Wide Wireless Web or WWW is being coined for this.

Set of 5G requirements

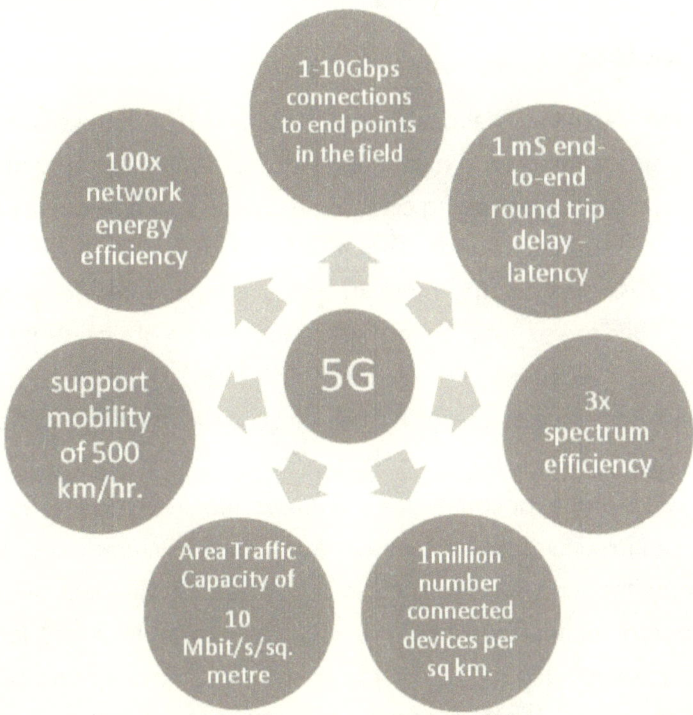

Figure 4.4: Visions for the Fifth Generation of Mobile Communications (Src - ITU)

Why do we need 5G ?

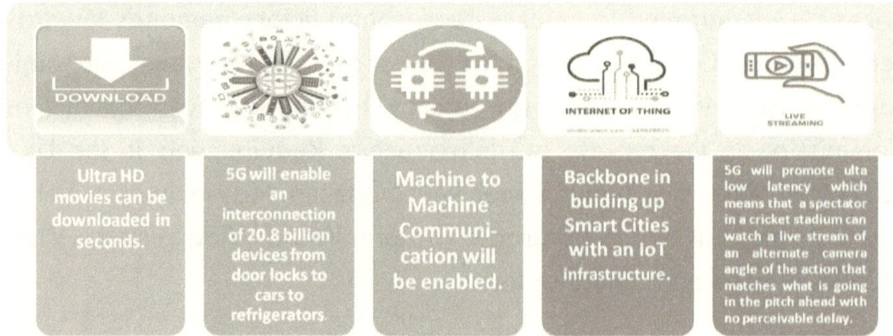

Figure 4.5

5G Technology

Millimeter Waves: Telecom Service Providers (TSPs) make use of radio frequency spectrum to send and receive data. With increasing number of consumers, more data is being consumed. But this data remains crammed on the same frequency bands. That means less bandwidth for everyone, causing slower service and more dropped connections. To avoid these problems, TSPs are experimenting with transmission of signals on a whole new swath of spectrum of 20~50 GHz. This band, acknowledged as the mmWave band, makes use of higher frequencies than the radio waves that have long been used for mobile phones. The mmWave band from 20~50 GHz alone accounts for 10 times more available bandwidth than the entire 4G cellular band.7Many manufacturers are fostering components that can be operated in the range of millimeter waves and semiconductor technologies that are suitable to operate at frequencies up to 90 GHz, especially in V-band (57 to 66 GHz) and E-band (71 to 86 GHz) applications. There is one disadvantage to the use of mmWaves, i.e. due to such high frequencies of mmWaves, they are not able to travel through buildings or obstacles and can be absorbed by foliage and rain.

Small Cells: Small cells can be placed throughout the cities after every 250 meters or so. They are portable miniature base stations that require minimal power to operate. Thousands of small cells installed in the city, due to the short range of mmWave signals, form a dense network called the HetNet (Heterogeneous Network) that receives signals from other base stations and send them to the users at different locations, like a relay. This largely prevents signals from being dropped. The term 'small cell' encompasses pico cells, micro cells, femtocells and can comprise of indoor/outdoor systems. Small cells can be as small as the size of a shoe-box. Such small cells can be bolted to light poles and the sides of buildings, hence do not require separate towers.

Massive MIMO: MIMO is the acronym for Multiple Input Multiple Output. MIMO refers to a wireless system that uses two or more transmitters and receivers to send and receive more data at once. Presently, 4G base stations possess a dozen ports for antennas to handle all cellular traffic. But 5G base stations can support about a hundred ports, which mean that a single array can accommodate many more antennas and hence can send to and receive signals from bountiful users at once. This leads to an increase in capacity of mobile networks by a factor of 22 or more. Below is a list of key technological characteristics of massive MIMO.

1. **Fully digital processing:** every antenna bears its own RF (Radio Frequency) and digital baseband chain. The signals emitted from all the antennas at each base station (due to MIMO) are processed coherently together. Fully digital processing allows to measure complete channel response on the uplink as well as quickly responds to such changes in the channel.

2. **Computationally inexpensive precoding / decoding:** As there are more than one transmitter and receiver in a MIMO network, there exists one LOS path from every transmitter to every receiver ideally. However, there may be reflection or diffraction from the surrounding atmosphere and the signals could interfere causing a low SNR (Signal to Noise Ratio) at the receiver. Hence the data streams cannot be decoded effectively. To avoid this precoding is used on the transmission side with the

goal of equalising the signal reception across multiple receiver antennas.

3. **Channel hardening:** Due to microscopic changes in environment, the channel gain tends to fluctuate randomly. This is known as channel fading. The channel is said to have hardened when the fluctuations in gain do not impact the transmitted data. Channel Hardening effectively removes the effects of channel fading. Operationally, each terminal-base station link forms a scalar channel whose gain stabilizes to a deterministic and frequency-independent constant.

4. The reliance on **reciprocity of propagation and TDD (Time division Duplex) operation** reciprocates the need for prior or structural knowledge of the downlink propagation channel since the downlink channels can be estimated from uplink pilots.

5. The array gain offers the link budget improvement and the spatial resolution of the array results in interference suppression. This facilitates the provision of **uniformly good quality of service to all terminals in a cell**.

Beamforming: Beamforming reduces the interference for nearby users by recognising the most efficient data delivery route from cellular base station to a particular user. Beamforming can help massive MIMO arrays for more skilled use of the spectrum around them. Massive MIMO faces a challenge to reduce interference while transmitting information from many antennas at once. At massive MIMO base stations, the best transmission route is plotted using signal-processing algorithms to send individual data packets in many different directions, bouncing them off buildings and other objects in a precisely coordinated pattern.

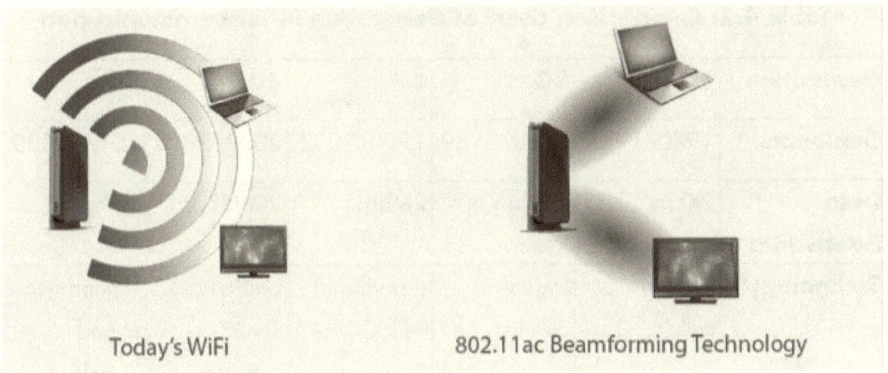

Figure 4.6: Visual representation of beamforming technology

Beamforming allows exchange of al lot of information between the users and antennas on a massive MIMO arrays by choreographing the packets' movements and arrival time.

Beamforming and the devices that support beamforming work under the IEEE 802.11ac specification.

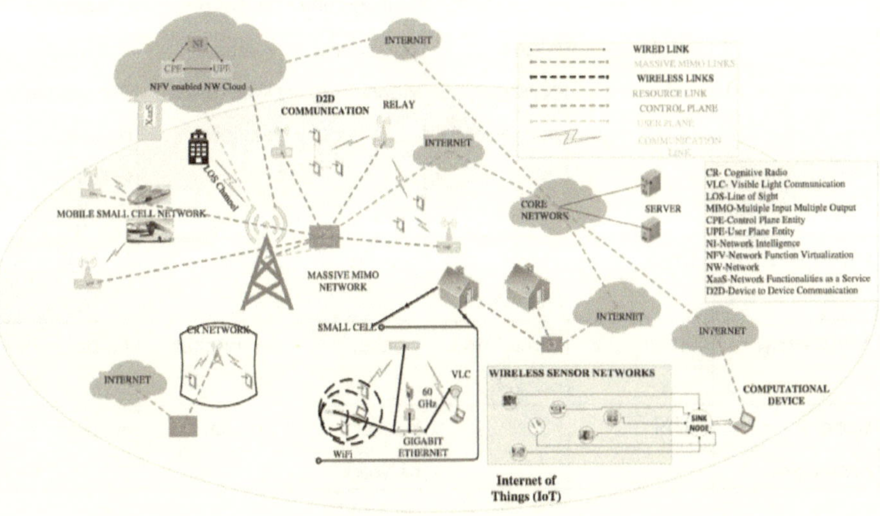

Figure 4.7: A General 5G Cellular Network Architecture

Source: *Akhil Gupta, Dr. Rakesh Kumar Jha; A Survey of 5G Network: Architecture and Emerging Technologies*

[9] **Table 4.2: Comparison chart of Generation in Telecommunication**

Generation	1G	2G	3G	4G	5G
Deployment	1970/1984	1980/1989	1990/2002	2000/2010	2017/2020
Data Bandwidth	2Kbps	14-64 Kbps	2Mbps	200Mbps	1Gbps
Technology	Analog cellular	Digital cellular	Broadband with CDMA, IP technology	Unified IP and seamless combination of broadband of LAN, WAN and WLAN	Unified IP and seamless combination of broadband, LAN, WAN, WLAN and WWWW
Services	Mobile technology (voice)	Digital Voice, SMS, Higher capacity packetized	Integrated high quality audio and video	Dynamic information Access, Wearable devices	Dynamic information Access, Wearable devices with AI capabilities
Multiplexing	FDMA	TDMA, CDMA	CDMA	CDMA	CDMA
Switching	Circuit	Circuit and packet	packet	All packet	All packet
Core Network	PSTN	PSTN	Packet network	Internet	Internet

Source: *Src- Hanamanta NB;5G wireless technology; CITECH; 2015)*

THE DISRUPTIVE ENTRY OF RELIANCE JIO WITH 4G TECHNOLOGY AND BUNDLE OF SERVICES IN INDIAN TELECOM MARKET

With its service Reliance Jio, the conglomerate has caused a big disruption in the Indian telecom market. As if the price war between Airtel, Vodafone, Idea, and Aircel wasn't bad enough, the launch of Jio has made competition even fiercer.

Reliance Jio is one of India's biggest network providers, and its marketing and business strategies have taken the world by storm. It had a major impact on revolutionising India's digital ecosystem. When it started doing business as a phone company in 2016, it had more than **50 million customers** in exactly 83 days. Focused on giving India the power of the digital revolution, which means connecting everyone by giving the best connectivity at the best price.

Mukesh Ambani started Reliance Jio Infocomm Limited, which is better known as Jio. It is now India's largest phone company. *Infotel Broadband Services Limited (IBSL)* was registered as a company in 2007. In 2010, Reliance Industries Limited bought 95% shares of IBSL. After this, IBSL changed its name to Reliance Jio Infocomm Limited, which is what it is now called.

The company opened for business in September 2016, and the most recent report from Telecom Regulatory Authority of India (TRAI) shows that it now has 398.31 million full-time subscribers.

Before Jio came along, there were more than 10 telecom companies operating on the market, but once it did, everything changed. Jio took the majority of the telecom industries with its low prices and cutting-edge technology. Companies like Aircel, MTS, Uninor (Telenor), etc., couldn't stay in business at the prices that Jio offered. Stronger companies like Airtel, Vodafone, and Idea were left in the market, and they are now Jio's competitor.

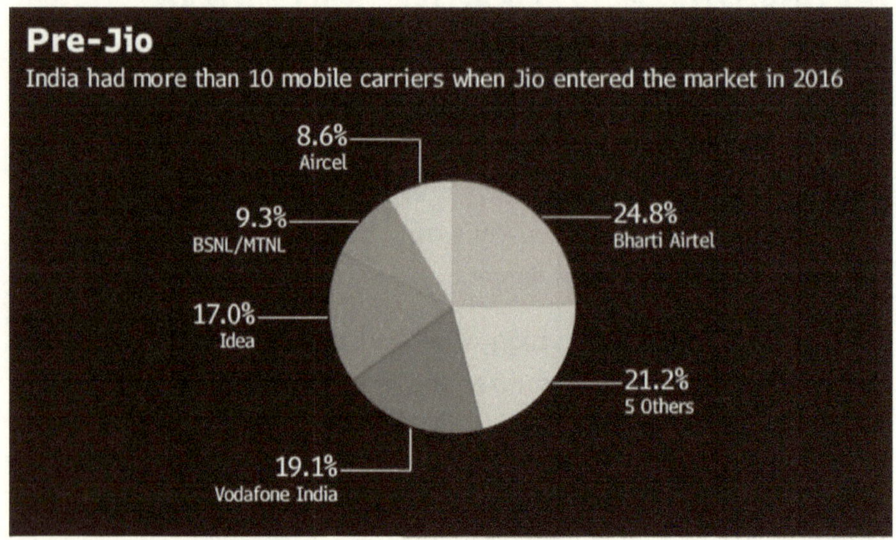

Figure 4.8: Reliance Jio Competitors (Pre- Jio)

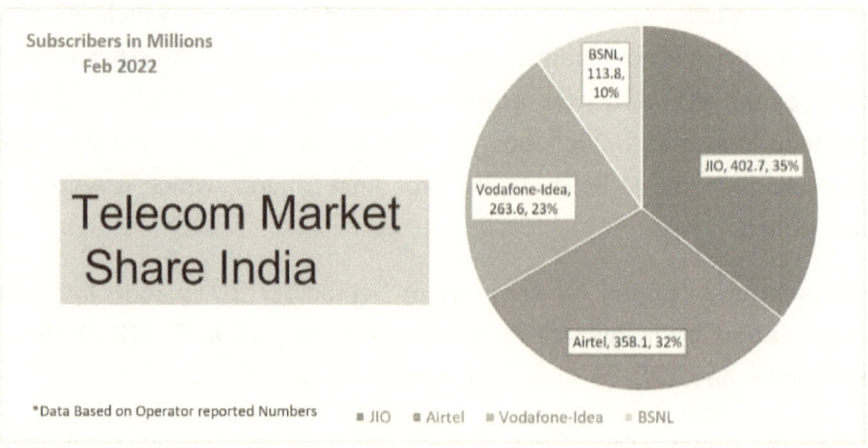

Figure 4.9

Source: *(Market Share of Telecom Industry as per Data by TRAI, February 2022)*

According to a report by TRAI from *February 2022*, Reliance Jio had the most subscribers with 35% of the market. Airtel and Vodafone-Idea (Vi) were next with 32% and 23%, respectively. As a public company, BSNL was able to stay in business and now has a 10% market share.

All of the other market players were suddenly overtaken by a new player, and the whole situation changed. This worked out even better for Jio. Before giving out the first SIM cards this year, when telecom services had been soft-launched, Jio spent more than Rs 1.3 trillion. The 4G phones made by LYF were also available at group stores. The first people to use (Reliance Jio Infocomme Ltd.) RJIL's voice and data services were Reliance Group employees, their families, and a few people who were invited. This was a few months ago. During this time, the Telecom Regulatory Authority of India (TRAI), RJIL, and the other mobile service operators had heated back-and-forth conversations. The other operators said that RJIL was getting unfair help from TRAI. It was clear that a price war was coming. And the operators who were already there, like Airtel, Idea, and Vodafone, cut their data prices before the launch because they thought RJIL would offer cheaper data prices.

Even though it took a long time to get ready, the launch on September 1, 2016, at the flagship company's annual general meeting was a big deal. RJIL's promoter Mukesh Ambani made a bold promise that RJIL's network, which is using the Voice Over Long-Term Evolution (VoLTE) technology, would always offer free voice calls, a large number of free SMSs, and free national roaming.

Also, RJIL is giving away all of its services for free until December 31, 2016. The company has issued 10 sample plans with different prices, ranging from Rs. 19 per day to Rs. 4,999 per month. In comparison to the terms of other operators' plans, RJIL's plans seem more generous because they offer more data at each price point. Users can also get free extra data between 2 a.m. and 5 a.m. and they can download data for free from RJIL Wi-Fi hotspots.

Through a variety of Jio-specific apps, the RJIL network also gives users access to large video libraries and many TV channels. For instance, the JioTV app has more than 300 live TV channels, JioMusic has more than 10 million songs, and JioCinema has TV shows, 6,000 movies, and more than 60,000 music videos.

The operator said that 4G data would cost an average of Rs 50 per GB, which is a lot less than the best deals offered by rival incumbents. But this would only be true for people who use hotspots to download data. Others paid an average of Rs 66 per GB for RJIL data, which was even very cheap at that time. RJIL also sells cheap phones and has made it clear that data used for VoLTE calls will not count toward the paid data that is included in the tariff plans. Data used for video calls, on the other hand, would be counted as paid-for data (everything is free until December 31, 2016, but the plans thereof, will kick in after that date).

Tariff plans were reviewed again in Jan 2017. By which time, RJIL aims to gain a large number of the 100 million users it was aiming for. Ambani has requested other operators to speedily handle mobile number portability requests because he thinks that many of these customers will be moving from other networks.

People who wanted to use the freebies during the test period waited in long lines outside of RJIL stores because of the launch offer. Reports say that there have been so many sign-ups that RJIL is having trouble getting enough SIM cards for everyone. Even though a network of 500,000 people was set up to move the goods, this happened. The RJIL IP-based network connects more than 18,000 urban areas over 200,000 villages.

RJIL says that Reliance Communications (RCOM) has transferred spectrum in the 800 MHz band to RJIL in 13 circles, and that RJIL and RCOM are sharing spectrum in the 800 MHz band in 21 circles. It also has spectrum in the 1800 MHz and 2300 MHz bands. RJIL wants to put more money into infrastructure and cover 90% of India's population by March 2017. When it comes to voice, RJIL subscribers have already lost a fair number of calls. Ambani says that so far, more than 50 million calls to numbers on other networks have been dropped (including the trial period of the soft launch). It is said that this is because the networks of other telecom operators are full. Also, there could be technical problems with how RJIL's VoLTE technology and the circuit switching technology used by different other networks connect to each other. A big point of disagreement between RJIL and other operators was how to connect their networks. When calls are made from one number on network A to another number on network B, the telecom operator of network A pays Rs 0.14 to the operator of network B per call to connect the two networks. RJIL has to pay this interconnectivity charge, and it gets the same amount when calls start on other networks and end on RJIL.

But as a new operator with few customers, RJIL will have to pay a lot more than it will get back, at least in the beginning. Since voice calls to other networks are free, it is paying for each one. Under these conditions, RJIL would gain a lot if interconnectivity fees were lowered or taken away. Reports say that TRAI is thinking about getting rid of these fees. But the move will be strongly opposed by operators who are already in the market. They believe it would give RJIL an unfair competitive advantage and cut into their profits.

Because of changes in the regulations about how to use the 4G spectrum, TRAI was once said to favour RJIL. Under the old TRAI rules, the LTW spectrum couldn't be used to offer voice over internet protocol (VoIP) services. This is precisely what VoLTE does. But this rule was later taken away, and VoIP, mobile virtual network operator (MVNO), as well as virtual private network (VPN) services, have all been allowed.

There has been a very public fight about how to connect things. The Cellular Operators Association of India, which is made up of companies like Idea, Vodafone, and Airtel, said that network traffic from RJIL's network is creating a "traffic imbalance" that is slowing down the network connections of all other operators, who are refusing to allow RJIL more Points of Interconnect (PoIs).

In fact, the current companies say that they weren't mandated by law to connect to RJIL. RJIL, in contrast, has said that the other telecom operators are attempting to harm its quality of service (QoS) through not letting points interconnect.

The TRAI is in charge of the interconnectivity problem, according to the Department of Telecommunications (DoT). So, it has refused to step in and asked the telecom operators to talk things out here with TRAI as a mediator. Since that time, Idea, Vodafone, and Airtel have indeed added more points of interconnection for RJIL.

The other operators have said that Jio's free voice call offer is "predatory pricing." This could change how business is done in the area. About 23–25% of the revenue from the Indian telecom market arrives from web traffic, while the rest comes from voice. The offer from RJIL turned this trend on its head. Even on a global scale, this was a new strategy because use of VoLTE data is usually paid for in other markets.

So, RJIL is betting a lot on its capability to make more people use data and give good service. All the Jio apps would therefore give access to multiple TV channels, electronic libraries of entertainment like films and songs, and other things like books, magazines, newspapers, newsfeeds, etc.

Its fact that the Reliance Group has already been involved in multiple news, media, as well as entertainment businesses, gives RJIL some confidence that it can get users to use more by providing them with content. In 2014, RIL bought Network 18, which has a lot of important attributes, such as CNBC-TV18, CNBC Awaaz, CNN-IBN, Firstpost, the entertainment channels like Colors, ETV portfolio, etc. This media takeover cost Rs 23 billion, and now Reliance Industries can use the material to get more users.

Even though their mobile data connections are slow and cause them to lag, Indians love to watch videos. As of now, about 45% of mobile data use was oriented by video, and that percentage was expected to rise to about 70% as internet consumption grew. In the next five years, the volume of data used for video is anticipated to go up 14 times. Because the Reliance Group is involved in the media, it has reason to think it knows how a persons use data and can try to get more persons to use it in a manner that a single telecom service provider can't. Also, the group may see RJIL as a loss leader to begin with (higher data consumption will benefit other group companies). If the strategy works in the long-term, it could be good for both Reliance and RJIL, since RJIL would begin to generate revenues and Reliance would make more money from entertainment and media.

But it's important to remember that RJIL's packaged media apps may also be brought into question because they may not follow the rules of network neutrality. This is because some media content on Jio apps is free, whereas other similar streaming episodes and videos may cost more money. We still don't know whether this will also be a big deal.

Irrespective of what happens, there is already a price war going on, and it will only get worse. To try to stop a lot of people from leaving, incumbents should offer the same thing as RJIL. As of now, it is not really clear that how well RJIL's plan will go. *Many people got a free SIM card, or maybe even a cheap phone, so they could use the services as long as they were free. If these users have a good experience, they may switch to paid services in the future.* The numbers won't be clear until January 2017, when the services will start to cost money.

Aside from price, the bar is low in terms of QoS right now, as users of other operators are unhappy with the percentage of dropped calls and network fadeout. If RJIL's quality of service (QoS) was good enough, anyone paying more than Rs 500 for voice and SMS right now might be tempted to switch to RJIL's Rs 499 plan or higher, depending on how much data they use. At the top of the market, competition will be about both price and quality of service (QoS).

There are also doubts about how well Reliance can serve retail customers. When RCOM was launched in 2002 by what was then the unified Reliance Group, it had similar deals like bundles of phones and deep price cuts. Even though RCOM did offer good value for money, they did not make the market share gains they had hoped for. This was because it couldn't take care of customers well. Customers complained about billing problems, slow responses to grievances, etc. So, the incumbents got more time to get back on their feet. Since then, people have been wondering if the Reliance Group can handle retail services. This time, things like SIM cards being out stock, slow activation, etc., have made these doubts even stronger.

Most users will probably "shop around" for rates at the lowest end of the scale. Everyone agreed that the most people will sign up for the service at the lower price points of Rs 149 and Rs 299. This is where existing operators will have to compete with the new service in terms of pricing. Jio seems to be acknowledging that the low-end market is heavily focused on voice. For example, the Rs 149 plan gives you 300 MB of data at a cost of Rs 496 for every GB (ignoring hotspot downloads).

RJIL probably hoped that low-income users would get hooked on using data during the free trial period and start paying for more overpriced data later on. Analysts of the media say that this could mean changing the way people think. Families with one cable TV subscriber would have to start thinking of their cell phones as their second and third "TV sets."

India has about 250 million smartphone users, but they don't use a lot of data (including about 70 million with VoLTE-capable handsets). The amount of data used each month was about 137 MB, and the RJIL Rs 149 plan gives you 300 MB. RJIL also says that during the soft-launch period, when about 1.5 million people were using the network, data usage surged to 26 GB per month and voice usage jumped to 355 minutes per month. Even though this sample was made up of people with higher incomes, it was clear that the amount of data being used could grow quickly.

ARPU, which includes both voice and data, is about Rs 192 for Airtel, the biggest operator that is still in business. CLSA, the largest brokerage and investment firm in Asia, says that even if RJIL gets an ARPU of Rs 250 and invests Rs 1.5 trillion, it will take about five years to break even, assuming a 10% return on capital employed before taxes. Even though the Reliance Group has put a lot of money into RJIL, it is only one of their businesses. As long as RJIL's established businesses, like refining and petrochemicals, keep bringing in a lot of cash, it can afford to get a piece of the telecom sector and wait for it to become profitable.

There is no doubt that RJIL has changed the way things work. After Jio came out, the share prices of companies like Airtel and Idea fell sharply. Analysts of stocks have cut their price goals for other publicly traded companies by 15% to 20%. As the market got used to the idea that the telecom arm could lose money for a long time, valuations and projections for Reliance Industries also went down.

EY's Global Telecommunication Leader, Prashant Singhal, says, "For a price-sensitive market like India, launch of cheap data services and free voice calls is a very good thing. This is likely to make more people use data. But the sector is struggling right now because it has a lot of debt and isn't making as much money as it used to. If data prices keep going down, it could hurt operators' ability to make money and stay in business. Telecom companies need to put more money into data networks. Any loss of market share at this point could affect how the upcoming spectrum auction goes, which is important for the Digital India vision.

In fact, there was concern that operators might not bid at all in the forthcoming spectrum auctions, which began on October 1, 2016, because they needed to save money and keep RJIL away. The government is selling 2,354.55 MHz of spectrum for a base price of Rs 5.56 trillion. The current mobile operators owe more than $61 billion, and ARPUs will go down after RJIL comes out. ICRA, a company that rates credit, says that operators' total debt grew by 41% between March 2014 & March 2016. Since RJIL came out, the real fight has been going on in TSPs.

CURRENT STATUS OF INDIAN TELECOM MARKET

As India heads into the last quarter of its 100th year as a free and independent country, the number of people who are connected to the internet is a key factor in boosting economic growth. During the month of June, 2.22 million more people in the country signed up for telephone service. Both the cities and the countryside saw growth.

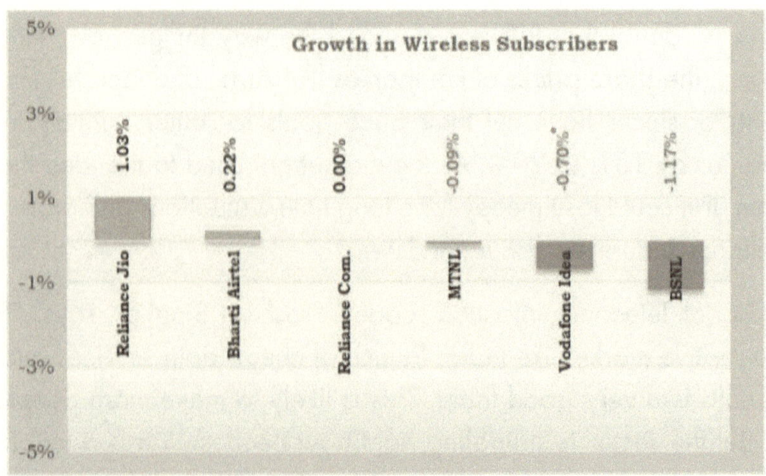

Note: BSNL includes its Virtual Network Operator (VNO).

Figure 4.10

Based on market share, 90% of subscribers chose private telecom companies, and the remaining 10% was split between BSNL and MTNL, which are both public companies.

Jio Subscribers in India

Compared to its competitors, Reliance Jio added a huge 4.22 million wireless customers in June. This means that there are now 413,01 million subscribers in total. The operator says that the number of low-paying customers has gone down while the number of smartphone users has gone up. This is mostly because of the low-cost Jio Phone Next smart phones.

Airtel SIM Users in India

On the one hand, while Reliance Jio was happy to add close to 4 million customers, Bharti Airtel had to be happy with just 0.79 million new wireless customers. This seems to show that the increase in tariff prices last winter had an effect. Airtel has 362.96 million customers right now.

Vi Subscribers in India

Vodafone Idea (Vi), unlike its rivals, lost about 1.8 million customers in June 2022. This was because it was still having trouble with 4G operations. Analysts are worried that if Vodafone Idea can't find a way out of its current cash crunch, the launch of 5G services by Jio and Airtel later this year will only make things worse for the cash-strapped operator.

State-owned telecom company **Bharat Sanchar Nigam Limited (BSNL)** also lost around a million customers in June, while MTNL lost a small number and Reliance Communications showed the same number as in May 2022.

However, Bharti Airtel has the most active subscribers, at around 98.41%. This means that of all the people who have signed up for its service, close to 98% are actually using it, while Reliance Jio has only 92.79%. Also, 85.2% of Vodafone Idea's customers were still using the service.

Moreover, the number of applications for Mobile Number Portability (MNP) rose to 9.02 million subscribers in June, which is a lot. Since MNP began, there have been 714,56 million requests for it.

WIRELESS SUBSCRIBERS IN INDIA

In terms of market share, Jio comfortably leads with a 36% market share. Airtel's market share improved slightly to reach 31.63%, while Vi's market share decreased to 22.37%. In all, private telecom players accounted for 90% of the market share in India's telecom industry in June 2022.

Access Service Provider-wise Market Shares in term of Wireless Subscribers as on 30th June, 2022

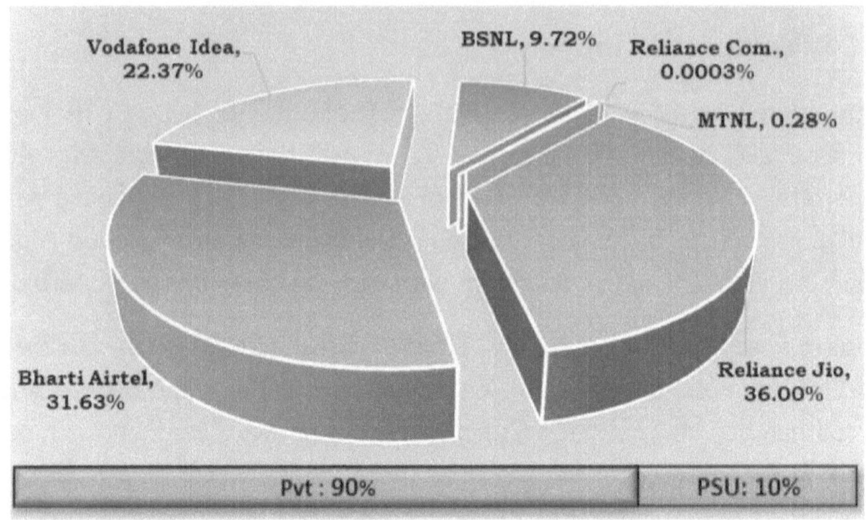

Figure 4.11: Market Share in terms of wireless subscribers

Total Broadband Subscribers in India

Even low-income families wanted a piece of the pie after the pandemic, which caused a wave of demand for broadband services. People across the country put education and work ahead of the cost of getting online. June was the same, as the number of broadband subscribers rose from 794 million in May to over 800 million in June. When we look at the number of people who use broadband, we can see that the fixed wireless segment, which includes Wi-Fi Max, Point-to-Point, and VSAT, grew the most over time. When it comes to the overall share of the market, Reliance Jio is again the leader with a huge 52.33 percent share. Bharti Airtel comes in second with a 27.39% share. Vodafone Idea had 15.35 percent of the market, and BSNL came in second with 3.12 percent.

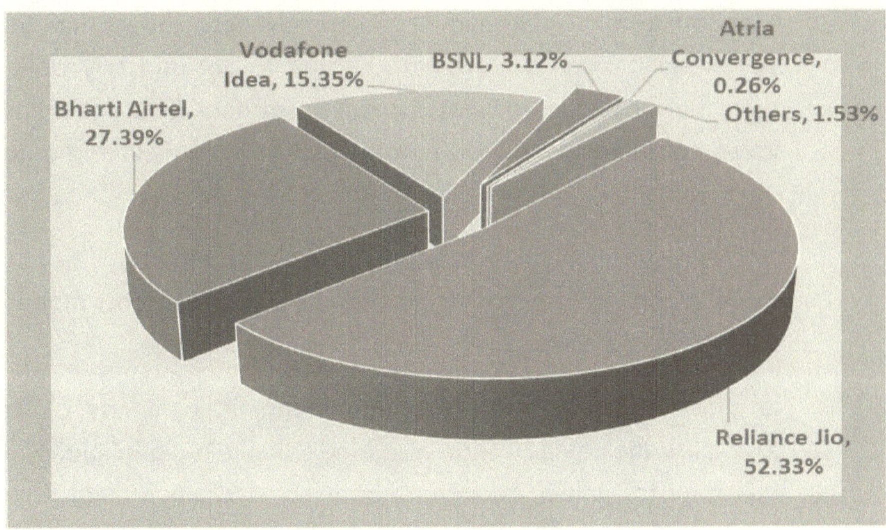

Figure 4.12: Service Provider-wise Market Share of Broadband (wired + wireless) Services as on 30th June, 2022

So, it's not too much of an exaggeration to say that Reliance has changed the game a lot with its free voice and cheap data packs, as well as its "basket of services" that complement and add to the basic mobile and Smartphone telephony. It also offers handsets as part of "bundled services," which means that customers can get both the device and the service.

Having said that, it should also be noted that Reliance is putting a lot of money into its venture and has already spent close to $2 billion on it. It is also taking the risk of "disruption with discounts," which might not work in the long run. In fact, its plan is to get as many subscriber bases as possible so that larger amounts can make up for razor-thin profit margins.

Highlights of Report of Institute of Competitiveness on Impact of Jio on Indian telecom industry

1. By making voice-based competition in to the data-based competition, Jio had been changed the way the Indian telecom industry looks.

2. A report from the Institute of Competitiveness shows that Jio has made it much easier and cheaper to get and buy data. Even the most conservative estimates say that Jio's entry has saved consumers Rs 60,000 crores a year just by making data cheaper.

3. Since Jio came out, it's easier and cheaper to get data. This has made us, in just six months, the country with the most mobile data users in the world.

4. To meet the different social and economic demands of its customers, the company had also tried to make a digital platform with apps for health, education, banking, and other things.

5. If everything else within the economy remains the same, an econometric analysis reveals that Jio's entry has accelerated India's GDP by more than 5.65%. This is because network effects are everywhere.

6. Since Jio entered in the Indian telecom market in Sept. 2016, a lot has changed in the industry. It changed how competition started working by giving its users free calls for life in a business where voice calls made up 75% of the money. Instead, data became the centre of competition. India became the nation with the most mobile data users around the world within 6 weeks of Jio's launch. India presently uses more than 1 billion Gigabytes of data every month, which is up from 200 million Gigabytes before Jio came out. According to Jio's most recent estimates, its users use an average of almost 10 Gigabytes of data, 700 minutes of voice calling and 134 hrs of video every month. One and a half years ago, this much digital use had never been seen before.

7. Reliance Jio's entry into the Indian telecom market had such a big impact that other telecom companies had to start focusing on strategies like acquisitions and mergers to deal with the tough

competition. At the end of April 2017, Jio had much more than 109 million customers. This made it challenging for other companies to compete. Brand names like Airtel, Vodafone, Idea, and BSNL had difficulty in making enough money in the country to remain profitable. Jio's plan to give away nearly all of its services for free has caused controversy in the market and made things hard for other network providers in India. As a result of Jio's entry, there is now a price war in the market.

POST DISRUPTION CHANGE IN VALUES & BENEFITS BEING OFFERED IN INDIAN TELECOM SECTOR

Reliance Jio's free voice calls as well as cheap 4G services changed the way people in India used data after it started selling services officially. This had a big effect on the telecom industry as a whole. The company's 4G data services were free for the first six months after launch, so customers could watch more online videos and other content than ever before. This became clear when India passed the US and China to become the world's biggest consumer of mobile data. Eventually, the company started charging for its services, but that didn't stop the Jio juggernaut. This was mostly because the company charged very little for its data, so many people signed up for its Jio Prime subscription service. Of course, Jio's competitors came up with plans that were just as good as Jio's, but they were cheaper and included more data and calls than before.

Here's 10 ways the telecom industry upgraded after Disruptive entry of Jio.

1. **Ultra-cheap data:** Before Reliance Jio came along, data was pretty pricey. On some networks, you had to pay up to Rs. 450 for 1GB of data. The best part of Jio's launch offer was that customers could get 4GB of high-speed 4G data per day for free. After that, they could keep getting data at 128kbps speed. After complaints from existing operators, the company had to come up with paid plans, but even then, the price was so low

that customers paid about Rs. 10 per GB of 4G data, which is what other operators started to do in response.

2. **Increased consumption of online content:** With free data, India saw a huge increase in the number of people who used the Internet. Jio says that in six months, India went from using 20 billion gigabytes of data to using 120 billion gigabytes of data. The company also says that the average consumer now uses 10 gigabytes of data per month.

3. **Free voice calls:** When Jio started up, voice calls became free for all users on all networks. The company has said that both local and long-distance calls to all networks will always be free on its network. In the end, competitors did the same thing by offering prepaid and postpaid plans with free minutes for both long-distance and local calls to all networks. Jio says that 250 billion minutes of calls are made every day on its network.

4. **Proliferation of 4G smartphones:** After Jio started offering services, the market for 4G smartphones exploded because everyone could use the company's 4G network for free. Since late 2015, there has been some interest in affordable 4G phones. After Jio, however, smartphones with 4G VoLTE started hitting the market for as little as Rs. 2,999. In fact, IDC and Morgan Stanley Research found that 95% of the smartphones sold across the country in the first quarter were 4G-ready.

5. **Faster mobile data:** Since most people were using 3G networks before 4G became the standard, mobile data speeds also went up. The latest data from TRAI's MySpeed app shows that Jio's average download speeds are around 18Mbps, while the incumbents' average download speeds are around 10Mbps.

6. **The death of 3G:** Since 2015, 4G has been the most talked-about thing in the telecommunications industry, but most operators still gave 3G speeds while upgrading to 4G. But since

Jio started doing business, the switch to 4G networks has moved faster, and 3G networks are ultimately being left behind. In fact, almost all phones sold today can connect to 4G networks.

7. **A record in user acquisition:** In February, Jio said that 100 million people had joined its telecom network in less than six months. Chairman Mukesh Ambani said at the time that this growth is even faster than what global giants like Facebook and WhatsApp have seen. There are 130 million users of Jio right now.

8. **Improved broadband Internet availability:** The telecoms regulator in India, TRAI, says that broadband speeds are anything above 512kbps. With the free Internet, millions of users got access to high-speed 4G networks, and Jio became the biggest provider of wireless Broadband in the country. This is even before the company's JioFiber service goes public, which it plans to do soon.

9. **Vodafone, Idea Cellular merged:** Vodafone and Idea Cellular, the country's second- and third-largest operators, announced a merger in March. Many people saw this as a way to fight back against Jio and its aggressive business practises. With the merger, the new company would have nearly 400 million users, 35 percent of the user market share, and 41 % of the revenue market share. It would be bigger than the current market leader, Airtel.

10. **Helped ease the way for online streaming services:** Jio says that each month, its network serves 165 billion hours of streaming videos. With this, the company's own JioTV app, the popular video-streaming service YouTube, and membership streaming services like Netflix, Amazon Prime Video, & Hotstar are likely to reach new audiences.

05

DISRUPTIVE INNOVATION STRATEGY OF RELIANCE JIO INFOCOMM LTD

Reliance Jio Infocomm Limited is a subsidiary of Reliance Jio platforms. It is an Indian company that works in telecommunications. Jio runs an LTE network that works all over the country and serves all 22 telecom circles. Jio has 4G and 4G+ services right now, but it wants to grow to 5G as well as 6G in the future. It has about 42.62 crores (426.2 million) members, making it India's largest mobile network operator and the third-largest in the world.

Jio has said that it will offer a service called "fibre-to-the-home" in September 2019. This service will include home broadband, TV, and phone services. As of September 2020, Reliance Industries has raised Rs.1.65 lakh crore (US$22 billion) by selling almost a third of its shares in Reliance Jio Platforms.

DIGITAL DISRUPTIVE BUSINESS STRATEGY OF RELIANCE JIO

1. AARRR Strategy of Reliance Jio

Reliance Jio's business plan is one of the main reasons why it has been so successful. When the AARRR strategy is used to break into the market, the company grows by a lot. This strategy has five key parts that will help a business find and keep customers in creative and cost-effective ways.

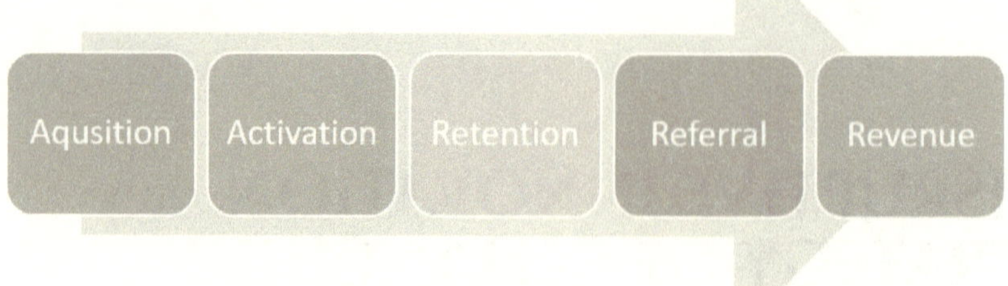

Figure 5.1: AARRR Strategy of Reliance Jio

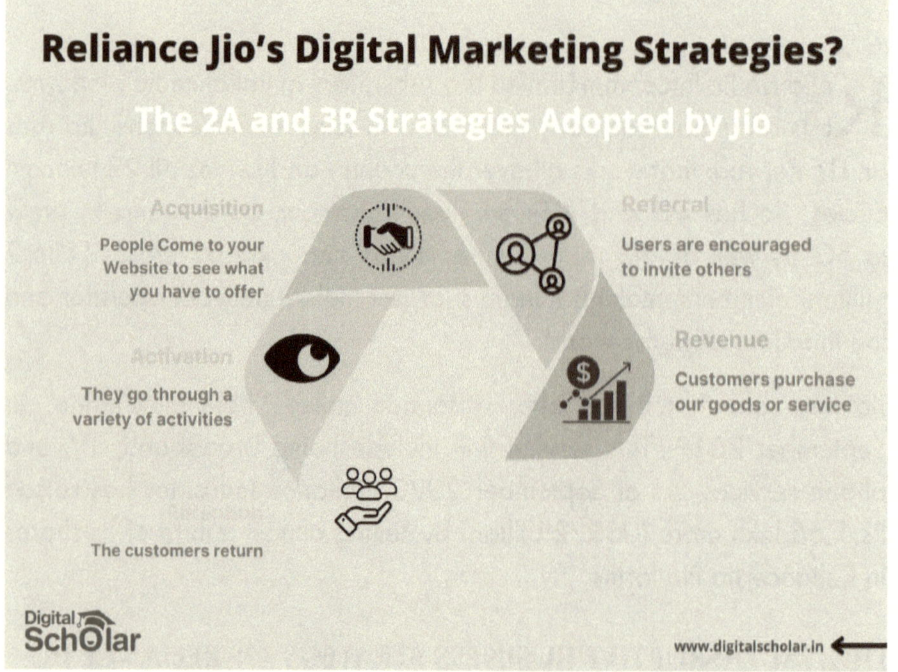

Figure 5.2: 2A and 3R Strategies by Jio

i. **Acquisition –** After Jio went commercial in September 2016, customers could use its services for free for three months. This plan was the best way for Jio to get people to sign up for their service. Jio was able to get 16 million customers in just one month.

ii. **Activation –** The users had the best experience ever, which was something that no other telecom service provider had ever done. Customers couldn't imagine having unlimited high-speed 4G data and unlimited calling, along with a bundle of free app services.

iii. **Retention –** Jio didn't stop here. On the first of the year 2017, they gave the users three more months of free services. Jio was the first company in history to give customers 6 months of free service. Jio has more than 300 million active customers after only two and a half years in business. It took its competitor, Bharti Airtel, more than 19 years to get to this number. That's how powerful Jio was.

iv. **Referral –** The people who bought it became its preacher. Jio kept getting more and more business because customers liked what they heard and how they used the service. This helped even more with its huge growth.

v. **Revenue –** Slashing the prices to 1/10th the existing cost, Jio got ahead with revenue, which was the major factor in getting such a leap in the market.

2. Moment Marketing

Jio has always been a major player when it comes to marketing in the moment, giving out trending content, & jumping on the bandwagon. Moment marketing is known for getting a lot of attention and being a hit with people who are always checking their feed for new and funny content.

3. Staying Local

Jio encourages Indian heritage in their social media messaging, staying true to the *Humara India* and *#VocalForLocal* culture that has grown over time. From wishing everyone a happy festival to creating material with

Indian themes and as much Bollywood as possible, the brand has taken a very wholesome Indian approach to its digital branding.

MARKETING MIX

According to Philip Kotler, "Marketing Mix is the mix of four elements, called the 4Ps (Product, Price, Place, and Promotion), that every company has the option of adding, subtracting, or modifying in order to create a desired marketing strategy."

i. **Product:** When we looked at what made Reliance Jio different from other companies in the Indian telecom market, it has been found the following:

- JIO only worked with 4G, but it could also work with 5G and 6G.
- JIO was based entirely on VoLTE, which meant that voice calls were made through the data network.
- Free voice calls, free data and free roaming were the main things that made Reliance JIO stand out.
- Users of JIO had a free welcome offer until the end of 2016. (it was extended till March, 2017). This came with free data, voice calls, and apps and content that could be useful. JIO used that time to teach users how to use JIO's features and fix interconnection problems with other networks. From a business point of view, it was done to quickly gain market share.
- With eKYC, customers were able to get their JIO SIM cards activated in 15 minutes. That is done with an Aadhar card. But this service was also offered by Airtel and Vodafone.

ii. **Price:** Reliance JIO has promised its customers that they will still get the cheapest data even after the welcome offer is over.

- Costs as low as Rs. 10-15 per GB. Reliance also gave 8 GB of Wi-Fi access at JIO Wi-Fi hotspots and unlimited use at night, so the price was definitely very fair.

iii. **Place:** Distribution channels had to be well thought out so that products could be sold. Even though JIO is a new company, its distribution strategy was set up so that it could reach 18000 cities and more than 200,000 villages across the country.

- JIO planned to have service in about 90% of India by March 2017. Reliance JIO planned to have about 1 million Wi-Fi hotspots by the middle of 2017. Users could get more data at Wi-Fi hotspots through their plans.

- Internet made available to Schools, colleges, and other public places through Wi-Fi (that was another strategy to motivate more users to switch to JIO).

iv. **Promotion:** Promotion is a big part of getting people to buy, and if the product is for the general public, there should be use of ATL (above-the-line) channels. Reliance Jio did a good job by making a plan before the launch of JIO in September 2016.

- In May 2014, Reliance paid about Rs. 4,000 to buy the TV18 network. Network18 owns many businesses, including TV channels like CNBC TV18, CNN-IBN, and CNN Awaz, websites like firstpost.com and moneycontrol.com, magazines like Forbes India, and entertainment channels like Colors, MTV, and Homeshop Entertainment.

- This enabled Reliance get effective level of coverage from media outlets like TV18 and others.

- As part of its plan to market itself, JIO made Shah Rukh Khan its brand ambassador. A lot of advertising was done through TV commercials, banners, hoardings, and print media. Social media promotion was also done on digital platforms.

- The brand's slogan was *"JIO Digital life,"* which was in line with the *#DigitalIndia* campaign of the Modi government. It also appealed to young people (18–35 years old) who use electronics and the internet in their daily lives.

- Everyone was surprised when Reliance Jio made a promising start in an industry where a strong market share was the only way to stay in business.
- Publicity was the most used tool in the promotional mix that wasn't advertising. To get more attention, JIO gave away free sim cards with free services. Since everyone likes free stuff, most people started purchasing JIO sim cards. By doing this, JIO got a lot of attention and set a record for getting more customers in a short amount of time. Any business that wants to be around for a long time needs to get the word out. This caused other operators' sales to go down, while JIO's sales went up.

TARGET AUDIENCE OF RELIANCE JIO

Reliance Jio wanted to offer the best and most affordable Internet services, so that they can focused on people with Smart Phones who need a fast internet service. Not only that, but 4G smartphones were the sole way to use their services, so they made people want them. Jio wants to attract both smartphone users and companies that require the use of digital technology. Bringing together merchants and the people who buy from them. Jio's plan is a one-of-a-kind way to get into any technology-based business. Some industries are education, Health Care, Media, and many others.

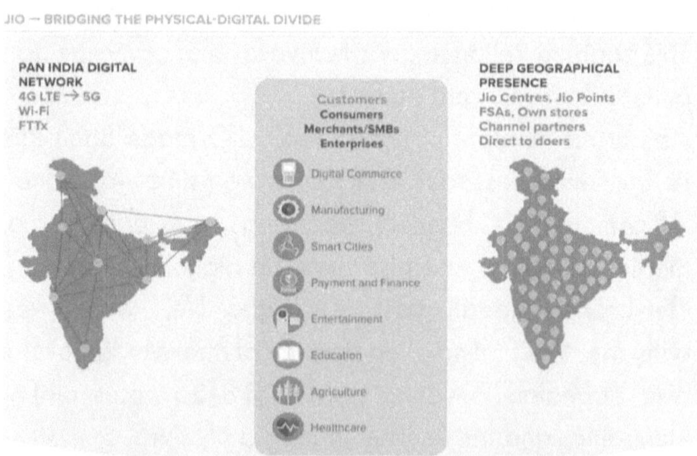

Figure 5.3: Target Audience of Reliance Jio

Digital Marketing Strategy of Reliance Jio for market penetration

Reliance Jio does a great job of digital marketing on most platforms because it has a great strategy and runs campaigns that are in style. On Instagram alone, it has more than 960k followers. Also, has a strong presence on YouTube, with more than 2.36 million subscribers and advertising campaigns in languages other than English. It is also active on Facebook, where more than 2.5 million people follow it. They have even more than 666k follower on Twitter, which is a lot less than their biggest competitor. Overall, Facebook and YouTube are their strong points, but they need to work on their Twitter. Reliance Jio has a digital strategy that is very good. Now is the time to look into Jio's social media strategy and digital marketing in more detail.

Because of its creative advertising campaigns, Reliance has been the focus of attention for the past few years. All mass media were used for these campaigns, which made us more interested in Jio's fast growth and low prices. Let's look at some of the most well-known campaigns.

FEW DIGITAL CAMPAIGNS OF JIO

i. Digital India, Home Delivered

Reliance Jio came up with a unique campaign by letting customers get their SIM cards sent to their homes. Customers didn't have to go out of their way to get their SIM Card from a store. Jio reached more than 26 million possible customers with this campaign in just 20 weeks. The Click- Through Rate (the number of clicks on a link divided by the number of times the link was seen) for this campaign was 0.72 percent, which was three times the average for the industry. Jio has set a very high bar with almost 30,000 leads per day.

ii. Jio Cheers Cricket

Reliance Jio never missed a chance to jump in when it came to India taking part in sports. A campaign called "Jio Cheers Cricket" was started to get more people excited about the India-Pakistan Match. The Thunderclap tool was built into the campaign, which helped it reach a huge number of people. As soon as *#JioforIndia* started getting a lot of attention on Facebook and Twitter, Jio sent notifications to their subscribers to get them involved.

- With an organic reach of more than 24.8 million
- more than 35,000 messages across platforms

Jio was the first company in India to do something like this on such a large scale. The number of people who filled out this scale was very high.

iii. Jio Cricket Play-Along

Cricket is among the most played sports in India. Jio knows how much fans care about the teams they sponsor in the Indian Premier League (IPL). Jio has come up with a way for cricket fans to win prizes every day by guessing the outcome of each ball played in a live cricket match. This is because Jio knows how much cricket fans love the sport. Jio's big marketing campaign won the "Best Use of Mobile Marketing" award at the 2019 Global Mobile (GLOMO) Awards at MWC19 in Barcelona.

PRICING EVOLUTION IN MOBILE NETWORK

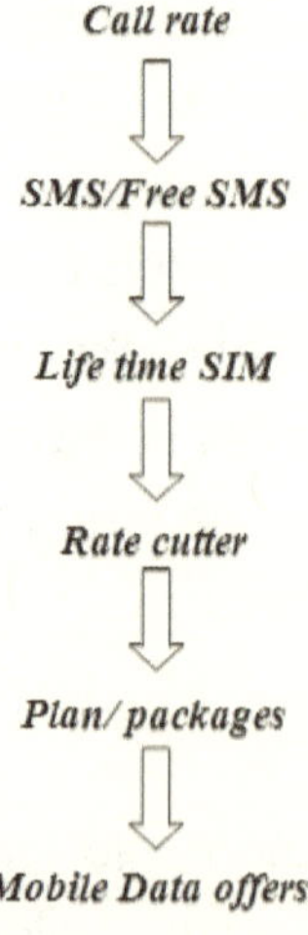

JIO's Offers at Introduction Level:

Launch of JIO into the market	Provide free SIM with registration of identity proof (only AADHAR) and mobile's bar code scanning of the user
Offers:	Unlimited voice calls; free SMS, *unlimited data* and free roaming.
Validity of offers:	5 months.

JIO's Offers at Second Level:

Availability of SIM in the market	Provide free SIM with registration of identity proof (only AADHAR).
Offers	Unlimited voice calls; free SMS, *4GB per day data* and free roaming.
Validity of offers	3 months.

JIO's Offers at Third Level:

Availability of SIM in the market	Provide free SIM with registration of identity proof (only AADHAR).
Offers	Unlimited voice calls; free SMS, 1GB per day data and free roaming.
Validity of offers	4 months

JIO's Offers at Fourth Level: JIO Prime Membership:

Existing Users	Users need to recharge Rs. 99 to get JIO Prime Membership to continue with already existing offers. Within a short period, they suddenly introduced *"JIO Dhan Dhana Dhan Offer"* where users need to recharge with Rs. 303 to continue their existing benefits for 3 month (90 Days)

New Users	A person who wants to buy a new Jio Sim first have to recharge with Rs. 99 to get Jio Prime membership and become a user of Jio. To get introduced *"Jio Dhan Dhana Dhan Offer"* new user recharge with Rs. 309 to get the service of Jio.

Table 5.1:

Source: *Salomi, I. S., & Selvan, G. (2017)*

Current Plans of JIO (2022)

The most popular plan of Jio is Rs 666 with Unlimited Calling any Net, 1.5GB/day Data, 100 SMS/ Day for 84 Days and Rs. 719 with Unlimited Calling any Net 2GB/day Data, 100 SMS/ Day for 84 Days with all the bundle of free subscription of Jio Apps.

Apart from the above Jio also launched Work from Home Data Pack during Lockdown period for the Working Class and Students for Online Classes.

SWOT ANALYSIS OF RELIANCE JIO

➤ STRENGTHS OF JIO

Strengths are characterised as what every corporate is best in its plethora of tasks, giving it an advantage over its competitors. They are an organization's inner strengths and assets that help it get good results and can be used to get ahead.

- **Most solid customer acquisition method:** Reliance Jio probably has the best customer acquisition method out there. For 3–6 months, the brand gave their services to all of their customers for free. This led to a lot of people using Reliance Jio, and it was one of the most impressive ways to get customers in the history of telecommunications.
- **Solid parent company:** Jio is a subsidiary of Reliance Industries Limited, which has a lot of money and can help Jio with its creative plans for the future. Dependence is a well-known

brand that is popular in India and has a high level of customer trust.

- **New technology:** Jio uses the latest 4G LTE technology, which is one of the best advances for the future in the world. This is made possible by Voice over LTE, which lets it work with 5G and 6G technologies, which are thought to be the future of long-distance communication.

- **Strong Customer Base:** In the first 170 days after its launch, Jio had 100 million customers, which is a record that no other provider has been able to beat. This has also made Reliance Jio the most well-known Internet service provider in India.

- **Market Share:** Being the first to offer information at a reasonable price gives you an edge. By getting a big share of the market, they forced other administrators to cut their prices.

➢ WEAKNESSES OF JIO

Weaknesses are inner traits and assets that stop a good result from happening. It is used to talk about areas where the business of an organisation needs to get better.

- **Late Entry:** Reliance Jio came late to the market, which was already filled with companies like Airtel and Vodafone that had a place in the minds of their customers. It is trying to build a piece of the industry as a whole, since its competitors are solid MNCs and money wouldn't stop them from keeping Jio in check.

- **Activation Issue:** Reliance Jio had a lot of problems getting started because it couldn't keep up with the huge number of customers it had. Such were the delays in activating the SIM card in the time after it was sent.

- **Reliance on data is high:** Since calls are free, Reliance Jio is very dependent on data charges.

➤ OPPORTUNITIES OF JIO

Opportunities are given to things on the outside that the substance can benefit from or use to help it reach its goals. These happen when a business can take advantage of its current situation to come up with and use methods that help it be more productive.

- **Future Driven Technology:** Reliance Jio uses VoLTE 4G service, which is flexible enough to work with 5G and 6G tech. This gives Jio a lot of options for how to expand its transmission capacity in the future.
- **Apps:** VoLTE, which is used by Reliance Jio, has a lot of bandwidth potential. So, they can sell apps that cost money or are free at first but cost money to use later.
- **Competitive Pricing Strategies:** Reliance Jio is proud to be a low-cost Internet service provider and a flexible manager. Since most of their competitors can›t afford their prices, this can help them target more markets and grow their market share.
- **Expansion:** Right now, Reliance Jio only works in India. Still, there is a lot of room for growth in foreign countries, especially those that are close by.
- **Data for Billion People:** The main chance comes from the data and how fast it comes in. Millennials are very active on many different platforms. The government's push for digitization is turning data from a luxury into a necessity.

➤ THREATS OF JIO

When conditions in the external environment put the business into the risk, this is called a threat. These outside factors could have a big effect on how well the project goes.

- **Risk of Losing Customers:** Customers tend to choose Jio because of the low prices they offer. At a time when the business is becoming more valuable, there may not be enough customers. Client devotion is a test.

- **Removal of Fee Services:** Jio is known for offering a lot of free services right now. If these are taken away, there may be less business for the company.
- **The Loyal Customer Base of Existing Players:** The current players have a strong presence on the lookout. People tend to stick with more stable and reliable service providers, making it hard for Jio to win over loyal customers of other service providers.
- **Criticism and Negative Image:** Ever since it started, Reliance Jio has been the subject of a lot of talk. The association now has a bad name because of these things.

"STATISTICAL ANALYSIS"

RELIABILITY AND VALIDITY OF RESEARCH INSTRUMENT

Table 5.2: Reliability Statistics

Cronbach's Alpha	Cronbach's Alpha Based on Standardized Items	N of Items
.844	.861	47

In this study referring to the above table it can be seen that Cronbach's alpha is 0.844, which indicates that a high level of internal consistency for the scale with this specific sample.

Table 5.3: Item-Total Reliability Statistics

	Scale Mean if Item Deleted	Scale Variance if Item Deleted	Corrected Item-Total Correlation	Squared Multiple Correlation	Cronbach's Alpha if Item Deleted
Age	114.1200	314.773	.034	.561	.846
Gender	114.7560	315.719	.036	.303	.844

	Scale Mean if Item Deleted	Scale Variance if Item Deleted	Corrected Item-Total Correlation	Squared Multiple Correlation	Cronbach's Alpha if Item Deleted
Educational Qualification	110.7600	311.974	.093	.455	.845
Occupation Status	112.6840	318.442	.077	.389	.853
Average Monthly Income	113.8920	313.486	.024	.554	.849
Locality	114.5200	313.793	.152	.255	.843
Current Telecom Service Provider	113.0720	313.063	.019	.315	.850
Type of Connection	114.7840	315.270	.011	.227	.846
Money spend on telecom service provider	113.8000	313.462	.060	.339	.846
Frequently switch to telecom service provider	112.0440	311.303	.084	.286	.846
Already changed the operator	113.4360	304.086	.271	.272	.842
Never changed the operator	112.1240	268.430	.389	.320	.848
Resistance to leave present operator I trust for	113.7600	302.143	.395	.447	.839
Strong sense of loyalty towards current telecom service provider	113.7920	297.804	.518	.529	.836

	Scale Mean if Item Deleted	Scale Variance if Item Deleted	Corrected Item-Total Correlation	Squared Multiple Correlation	Cronbach's Alpha if Item Deleted
Shopping for new telecom service provider is too much problematic	113.5600	299.187	.474	.552	.837
As telecom service providers are focusing only on short term offering to attract customers	113.9640	303.906	.348	.454	.840
Difficult to make comparisons b/w telecom service providers	113.7280	297.661	.521	.578	.836
I don't have much time to research for telecom service provider selection	113.7800	298.421	.520	.586	.836
I don't want to lose current deal/package	113.6600	296.780	.544	.473	.836
I feel big risk that something will gowrong in switching	113.3600	292.207	.615	.735	.834
I don't know enough to make a right choice	113.3480	292.123	.627	.718	.833

	Scale Mean if Item Deleted	Scale Variance if Item Deleted	Corrected Item-Total Correlation	Squared Multiple Correlation	Cronbach's Alpha if Item Deleted
I feel out-of-date when I talk to sales staff	113.3680	295.101	.564	.719	.835
There is no difference in cost of telecom service supplier	113.6000	298.498	.466	.619	.837
There is no difference in quality of telecom service supplier	113.4320	297.419	.499	.608	.836
Don't know where to find trusted info about available options	113.5360	295.768	.526	.561	.836
Wide 4G Connectivity	114.4720	306.170	.339	.608	.840
High Speed Internet	114.3840	305.217	.363	.705	.840
Discounted and Unlimited Data Tariff	114.2000	303.285	.371	.650	.839
Unlimited HD Voice Calls	114.2640	305.376	.354	.698	.840
Free Apps subscription	113.9640	299.039	.456	.627	.837
Disruptive Pricing Strategy	114.0400	299.749	.462	.571	.838
Reliance Jio	114.1200	302.259	.436	.360	.838
Vodafone Idea Vi	113.4320	303.901	.344	.459	.840
Airterl	113.7920	304.985	.311	.314	.841

	Scale Mean if Item Deleted	Scale Variance if Item Deleted	Corrected Item-Total Correlation	Squared Multiple Correlation	Cronbach's Alpha if Item Deleted
BSNL	113.3000	301.745	.389	.464	.839
Reliance Jio	114.2880	312.873	.110	.235	.844
Vodafone Idea Vi	114.1160	310.553	.214	.354	.842
Airtel	114.2880	312.037	.142	.248	.844
BSNL	114.0800	312.757	.114	.349	.844
How much satisfied are you with the communication of executives of your telecom service provider's ?	113.9320	304.546	.382	.625	.840
How much satisfied are you with the services of the Sales Department of your telecom service provider?	113.7520	302.525	.437	.669	.838
Are you satisfied with the network availability in your area?	113.7680	303.641	.333	.624	.840
Are you satisfied with (Value Added Services) VAS services provided by your service provider?	113.6440	302.704	.424	.515	.839

	Scale Mean if Item Deleted	Scale Variance if Item Deleted	Corrected Item-Total Correlation	Squared Multiple Correlation	Cronbach's Alpha if Item Deleted
Are you satisfied with 2G, 3G and 4G internet facility of your service provider?	113.8440	303.594	.381	.666	.839
Are you satisfied with online services provided at your service provider's website?	113.8800	304.821	.382	.611	.840
Are you satisfied more with current network comparatively with other network?	113.9600	314.553	.040	.168	.846
Are you satisfied with network availability while travelling?	113.5120	304.669	.312	.496	.841

Source: *Survey Data*

The above table presents the value that Cronbach's alpha would be if that particular item was deleted from the scale. We can see that removal of questions, whose Corrected Item-Total Correlation values are less than .05, would result in a lower Cronbach's alpha. Therefore, we did not remove these questions.

1. **VALIDITY:** Research validity in surveys relates to the extent at which the survey measures right elements that need to

be measured. In simple terms, validity refers to how well an instrument as measures what it is intended to measure. Validity explains how well the collected data covers the actual area of investigation (Ghauri and Gronhaug, 2005). Validity basically means "measure what is intended to be measured" (Field, 2005).

Validity Analysis

Based on the validity analysis output in mind some values like Pearson Correlation or Correlation value between of the different items or the item with the total score also known as Sig. (2-tailed) was significant level of 5%, while N is the total survey respondents is 250 people. As explained in the validity analysis and based on the significant value obtained by the Sig. (2-tailed) of 0.000 in the case of maximum items of the questionnaire is <0.05, so it can be concluded that all items are valid. (Data Sheet Attached in Appendix)

DATA ANALYSIS & INTERPRETATION

This section of the chapter sets out the descriptive statistics. As noted in the previous chapter, the research population comprised 300 research participants, but only 250 valid respondents were received, and electronic method of data collection in order to ensure there was maximum data collection using a purposive sampling approach

Table 5.4: Age and Educational Qualification Cross tabulation

			Educational Qualification						Total
			Primary	High School	Intermediate	Graduation	Post-Graduation	PhD	
Age	Below 20	Count	0	4	35	22	1	0	62
		% of Total	0.0%	1.6%	14.0%	8.8%	0.4%	0.0%	24.8%
	20-30	Count	0	1	8	39	70	14	132
		% of Total	0.0%	0.4%	3.2%	15.6%	28.0%	5.6%	52.8%

			Educational Qualification						Total
			Primary	High School	Intermediate	Graduation	Post-Graduation	PhD	
31-40		Count	2	0	0	6	22	13	43
		% of Total	0.8%	0.0%	0.0%	2.4%	8.8%	5.2%	17.2%
41-50		Count	1	0	0	1	4	3	9
		% of Total	0.4%	0.0%	0.0%	0.4%	1.6%	1.2%	3.6%
51-60		Count	0	0	0	0	0	2	2
		% of Total	0.0%	0.0%	0.0%	0.0%	0.0%	0.8%	0.8%
61 and above		Count	0	0	0	0	0	2	2
		% of Total	0.0%	0.0%	0.0%	0.0%	0.0%	0.8%	0.8%
Total		Count	3	5	43	68	97	34	250
		% of Total	1.2%	2.0%	17.2%	27.2%	38.8%	13.6%	100.0%

Source: *Own findings*

Table 5.4 shows the educational qualifications of the respondents on the basis of age groups. The table highlighted respondents between the 20-30 were highly qualified in comparison to the other age groups. 28.0% **(70)** of the respondents in the age group of 20-30 have passed their Post-Graduation, 15.6% **(39)** have a graduation degree and 5.6% **(14)** of the respondents were Doctorate.

Table 5.5: Age and Occupation Status Cross tabulation

			Occupation Status						Total
			Unemployed	Employed	Retired	Business	Student	Other	
Age	Below 20	Count	6	0	0	0	56	0	62
		% of Total	2.4%	0.0%	0.0%	0.0%	22.4%	0.0%	24.8%
	20-30	**Count**	**12**	**58**	**0**	**2**	**60**	**0**	**132**
		% of Total	**4.8%**	**23.2%**	**0.0%**	**0.8%**	**24.0%**	**0.0%**	**52.8%**

			Occupation Status						Total
			Unemployed	Employed	Retired	Business	Student	Other	
31-40		Count	2	30	0	4	6	1	43
		% of Total	0.8%	12.0%	0.0%	1.6%	2.4%	0.4%	17.2%
41-50		Count	0	6	0	2	0	1	9
		% of Total	0.0%	2.4%	0.0%	0.8%	0.0%	0.4%	3.6%
51-60		Count	0	2	0	0	0	0	2
		% of Total	0.0%	0.8%	0.0%	0.0%	0.0%	0.0%	0.8%
61 and above		Count	0	0	2	0	0	0	2
		% of Total	0.0%	0.0%	0.8%	0.0%	0.0%	0.0%	0.8%
Total		Count	20	96	2	8	122	2	250
		% of Total	8.0%	38.4%	0.8%	3.2%	48.8%	0.8%	100.0%

Source: *Own findings*

The above table 5.5 reflects the occupation status of the respondents on the basis of age groups and reveals that 23.2% **(58)** were employed and 24.0% **(60)** were students between the age of 20-30. The respondents from the other groups were comparatively low in terms of employment, student, and other categories.

Table 5.6: Age and Average Monthly Income Cross tabulation

			Average Monthly Income					Total
			Less than 10,000	10,000-25,000	25,000-50,000	50,000-1,00,000	More than 1,00,000	
Age	Below 20	Count	50	7	5	0	0	62
		% of Total	20.0%	2.8%	2.0%	0.0%	0.0%	24.8%
	20-30	**Count**	**57**	**26**	**26**	**15**	**8**	**132**
		% of Total	**22.8%**	**10.4%**	**10.4%**	**6.0%**	**3.2%**	**52.8%**
	31-40	Count	3	5	11	12	12	43
		% of Total	1.2%	2.0%	4.4%	4.8%	4.8%	17.2%
	41-50	Count	1	1	0	6	1	9
		% of Total	0.4%	0.4%	0.0%	2.4%	0.4%	3.6%

			Average Monthly Income					Total
			Less than 10,000	10,000-25,000	25,000-50,000	50,000-1,00,000	More than 1,00,000	
	51-60	Count	0	0	0	0	2	2
		% of Total	0.0%	0.0%	0.0%	0.0%	0.8%	0.8%
	61 and above	Count	0	0	0	2	0	2
		% of Total	0.0%	0.0%	0.0%	0.8%	0.0%	0.8%
Total		Count	111	39	42	35	23	250
		% of Total	44.4%	15.6%	16.8%	14.0%	9.2%	100.0%

Source: *Own findings*

Table 5.6 represents the average monthly income of the respondents from different age groups and highlights that 22.8% **(57)** respondents were earning less than 10,000 per month from the age group of 20-30. 10.4% **(26)** of the respondents from the same age group fall under the category of 10,000-25,000 and 25,000-50,000 average monthly income respectively. The above table also reveals that respondents of the same category earned comparatively high in comparison to the respondents from other different age groups.

Table 5.7: Age and Locality Cross tabulation

				Locality		Total
				Rural	Urban	
Age	Below 20		Count	29	33	62
			% of Total	11.6%	13.2%	24.8%
	20-30		**Count**	**45**	**87**	**132**
			% of Total	**18.0%**	**34.8%**	**52.8%**
	31-40		Count	8	35	43
			% of Total	3.2%	14.0%	17.2%
	41-50		Count	3	6	9
			% of Total	1.2%	2.4%	3.6%
	51-60		Count	1	1	2
			% of Total	0.4%	0.4%	0.8%
	61 and above		Count	1	1	2
			% of Total	0.4%	0.4%	0.8%
Total			Count	87	163	250
			% of Total	34.8%	65.2%	100.0%

Table 5.7 highlights the locality of the different age group respondents. As per the data collected data table reveals that the majority of the respondents from the age group of 20-30 belong to the urban background 34.8% **(87)** and 18.0% **(45)** belong to the rural background.

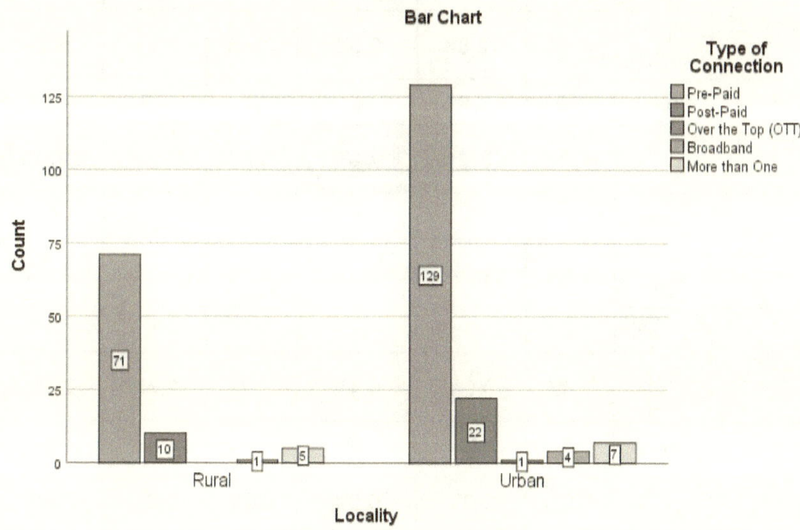

Chart 5.4:

Source: *Own Findings*

The above chart 5.4 reflects the types of connections used by the respondents on the basis of locality. It reflects that maximum number of respondents **(129)** were using pre-paid connection in the urban area, whereas, in rural area the total number of pre-paid connection users were only **(71)**.

Table 5.8: Age * Current Telecom Service Provider Cross tabulation

			Current Telecom Service Provider					Total
			Airtel	Reliance Jio	Vodafone-Idea (Vi)	BSNL/ MTNL	Other (more than one)	
Age	Below 20	Count	11	32	5	1	13	62
		% of Total	4.4%	12.8%	2.0%	0.4%	5.2%	24.8%
	20-30	**Count**	**16**	**58**	**6**	**3**	**49**	**132**
		% of Total	**6.4%**	**23.2%**	**2.4%**	**1.2%**	**19.6%**	**52.8%**
	31-40	Count	6	9	5	0	23	43
		% of Total	2.4%	3.6%	2.0%	0.0%	9.2%	17.2%
	41-50	Count	2	0	1	0	6	9
		% of Total	0.8%	0.0%	0.4%	0.0%	2.4%	3.6%
	51-60	Count	0	0	0	0	2	2
		% of Total	0.0%	0.0%	0.0%	0.0%	0.8%	0.8%
	61 and above	Count	0	0	0	0	2	2
		% of Total	0.0%	0.0%	0.0%	0.0%	0.8%	0.8%
Total		Count	35	99	17	4	95	250
		% of Total	14.0%	39.6%	6.8%	1.6%	38.0%	100.0%

Source: *Own findings*

Table 5.8 reflects the users of the different telecom service providers on the basis of respondents' age groups. The table reveals that the majority of the respondents fall under the age group of 20-30 **(132)**. According to the data collected, 6.4% **(16)** of the respondents in the same age group were using Airtel, 23.2% **(58)** were using Reliance Jio, and 2.4% **(6)**, 1.2% **(3)**, and 19.6% **(49)** were using Vodafone-Idea, BSNL/ MTNL, and more than one service respectively. Another highest number of responses was recorded in the category of Below 20 i.e., Airtel 4.4%

(11), Reliance Jio 12.8% **(32)**, Vodafone-Idea 2.0% **(5)**, BSNL / MTNL 0.4% **(1)**, and Other 5.2% **(13)**.

Table 5.9: Gender * Current Telecom Service Provider Cross tabulation

			Current Telecom Service Provider					Total
			Airtel	Reliance Jio	Vodafone-Idea (Vi)	BSNL/ MTNL	Other	
Gender	Male	Count	18	**55**	11	1	61	**146**
		% of Total	7.2%	**22.0%**	4.4%	0.4%	24.4%	**58.4%**
	Female	Count	17	**44**	6	3	34	**104**
		% of Total	6.8%	**17.6%**	2.4%	1.2%	13.6%	**41.6%**
Total		Count	35	99	17	4	95	250
		% of Total	14.0%	39.6%	6.8%	1.6%	38.0%	100.0%

Source: *Own findings*

The above table 5.9 reflects the usage of different telecom services on the basis of the gender of the respondents and highlights that, male respondents were using the maximum number of telecom services 58.4% **(146)** in comparison to the female users 41.6% **(104)**. The table also revealed that the maximum number of users in both genders was using Reliance Jio i.e., 22.0% **(55)** in the male category and 17.6% **(44)** in the female category.

Table 5.10: Locality * Current Telecom Service Provider Cross tabulation

			Current Telecom Service Provider					Total
			Airtel	Reliance Jio	Vodafone-Idea (Vi)	BSNL/ MTNL	Other	
Locality	Rural	Count	15	**37**	4	2	29	**87**
		% of Total	6.0%	**14.8%**	1.6%	0.8%	11.6%	**34.8%**
	Urban	Count	20	**62**	13	2	66	**163**
		% of Total	8.0%	**24.8%**	5.2%	0.8%	26.4%	**65.2%**
Total		Count	35	99	17	4	95	250
		% of Total	14.0%	39.6%	6.8%	1.6%	38.0%	100.0%

Source: *Own findings*

The above table 5.10 shows that out of a total of 250 respondents 65.2% **(163)** belong to the urban area and 34.8% **(87)** belong to the rural area of the region. The table also reflected that 26.4% **(66)** of respondents were users of more than one telecom service provider in the urban area including Reliance Jio as one service by 24.8% **(62)** whereas in the rural part majority of the respondents i.e., 14.8% **(37)** were using Reliance Jio.

Table 5.11: Locality * Average Monthly Income Cross tabulation

Count							
		Average Monthly Income					Total
		Less than 10,000	10,000-25,000	25,000-50,000	50,000-1,00,000	5.00	
Locality	Rural	43	14	16	10	4	87
	Urban	**68**	**25**	**26**	**25**	**19**	**163**
Total		111	39	42	35	23	250

Source: *Own findings*

Table 5.11 reflects the average monthly income of the respondents belonging to the rural and urban areas of the study region and highlights that respondent from an urban area is having more average monthly income in all the different categories in comparison to the rural area respondents.

Table 5.12: Average Monthly Income * Money spent on telecom service provider Cross tabulation

Count							
		Money spent on the telecom service provider					Total
		Less than 200	200-500	500-700	700-1,000	More than 1,000	
Average Monthly Income	Less than 10,000	25	**65**	12	6	3	111
	10,000-25,000	7	20	7	4	1	39
	25,000-50,000	1	20	16	4	1	42
	50,000-1,00,000	1	17	12	2	3	35
	More than 1,00,000	2	9	3	4	**5**	23
Total		36	131	50	20	13	250

Source: *Own findings*

Table 5.12 represents the money spent on telecom services on the basis of the respondents' average monthly income. In the category of less than 10,000 average monthly income, maximum respondents were spending Rs. 200-500 for availing of telecom services whereas the respondents earning more than 1,00,000 were spending more than Rs. 1,000 on telecom services in comparison to the other respondents from different average monthly income categories.

Table 5.13: Locality * Money spent on telecom service provider Cross tabulation

Count							
		Money spent on the telecom service provider					Total
		Less than 200	200-500	500-700	700-1000	More than 1000	
Locality	Rural	15	40	22	7	3	87
	Urban	**21**	**91**	**28**	**13**	**10**	**163**
Total		36	131	50	20	13	250

Source: *Own findings*

Table 5.13 reveals that on the basis of the locality the maximum number of the respondents from urban areas spent more money on telecom services. The rationale explanation behind the same can be easily understood with the help of **table 7** which reveals that the maximum number of users i.e., 65.2% **(163)** belong to the urban area, and also from **table 8** which reveals that the average monthly income of the respondents from an urban area is on a higher side in comparison to the respondents from the rural area.

Table 5.14: Current Telecom Service Provider * Frequently switch to telecom service provider Cross tabulation

			Frequently switch to the telecom service provider					Total
			Within a year	Once a year	In two years once	In two to five years once	Not at all	
Current Telecom Service Provider	Airtel	Count	3	2	4	4	22	35
		Expected Count	2.9	1.7	2.9	7.8	19.6	35.0
	Reliance Jio	Count	9	3	9	17	**61**	**99**
		Expected Count	8.3	4.8	8.3	22.2	55.4	99.0
	Vodafone-Idea (Vi)	Count	2	1	1	4	9	17
		Expected Count	1.4	.8	1.4	3.8	9.5	17.0
	BSNL/ MTNL	Count	1	0	0	0	3	4
		Expected Count	.3	.2	.3	.9	2.2	4.0
	Other (More than one)	Count	6	6	7	31	45	95
		Expected Count	8.0	4.6	8.0	21.3	53.2	95.0
Total		Count	21	12	21	56	140	250
		Expected Count	21.0	12.0	21.0	56.0	140.0	250.0

Source: *Own findings*

Table 5.14 provides descriptive statistics and cross tabulation between the current telecom and the frequency to switch the telecom service provider. The analysis reflects that the maximum number of Reliance Jio users never changed the telecom service i.e., **61**, and the majority of the Reliance Jio users are comparatively high which **99** with other service providers are.

Table 5.15: Correlations

		Current Telecom Service Provider	Never changed the operator
Current Telecom Service Provider	Pearson Correlation	1	**.106***
	Sig. (1-tailed)		.047
	N	250	250
Never changed the operator	Pearson Correlation	.106*	1
	Sig. (1-tailed)	**.047**	
	N	250	250
*. Correlation is significant at the 0.05 level (1-tailed).			

Source: *Own findings*

Based on above table 5.15, we can state that never changed the operator and current telecom service provider have a statistically significant linear relationship **(r=.106, p<.05)**. The direction of the relationship is positive between these variables and tends to increase together.

Null Hypothesis-1 (Qualitative): Disruptive Innovation Strategy has no difference from Evolutionary and Revolutionary Innovation Strategy *(Result: Null Hypothesis Rejected*

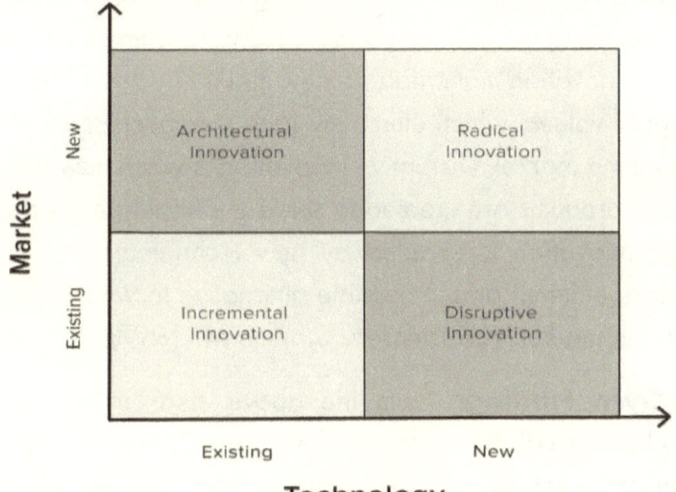

Figure 5.5: The Innovation Matrix

- **Evolutionary Innovation:** Is an Incremental / Sustaining Innovation that talks about continuous improvement of existing products or services to provide more value to an existing market. It focuses on reducing defects and incrementally improving performance with features like product line expansions, cost reductions, and next-generation products. *(F.Dieffenbacher, 2022)*

- **Revolutionary (discontinuous / radical) Innovation:** Revolutionary innovation refers to the co-occurrence of a radical new mindset and radical new technology. These "new to the world" or game-changing innovations move organizations into uncharted technological and cognitive waters. This implies that organizations aiming for revolutionary innovation have to break away from existing technological assumptions and normal sensemaking, and create new mental models of how to approach the market while at the same time reinventing existing technological solutions. *(Ringberg, T., Reihlen, M., & Rydén, P. 2019).*

- **Disruptive Innovation:** 'Disruptive Innovation' refers to an innovation that creates a fundamentally new value network. This can be achieved by either creating a new market or by entering an existing market and changing how consumers interact with it. An innovation that creates a new market by providing a different set of values, which ultimately (and unexpectedly) overtakes an existing market. Disruptive innovation is when new technologies and products are created to serve an existing market. This type of innovation is enabled by new technology that provides a more efficient and accessible alternative to what already exists in the market. *(Christensen, Clayton M. 1997)*

Source Own Finding: From the above clear-cut demarcation of difference between all three aforesaid mentioned innovations. Disruptive Innovation is eventually varied different from the Evolutionary and Revolutionary Innovation on the basis of degree of uses of new technology and degree of newness of the market. So, from the above discussion of available literature, **Null Hypothesis is being rejected.**

Null Hypothesis 2: Disruptive innovation has no effect on new markets and new products or services *(Result: Null Hypothesis Rejected)*

Table 5.10 above reflects that the majority of the Reliance Jio users in both localities were high because the services offered by the company are as per the expectations of the users. Table 13a supports the results by representing that the maximum number of the respondents never changed the operator because the current operator is providing better innovative and disruptive offers to the users.

Table 5.16a: Never changed the operator

	Observed N	Expected N	Residual
Satisfied with the current operator	87	27.8	59.2
Most of my contact persons are clients of the current operator	28	27.8	.2
Offers the best prices	24	27.8	-3.8
The switching process is too complicated	7	27.8	-20.8
The decision of another person	2	27.8	-25.8
Better network coverage	40	27.8	12.2
Want to keep the same number	17	27.8	-10.8
Brand loyalty	5	27.8	-22.8
Other	40	27.8	12.2
Total	250		

Source: *Own findings*

Table 5.16b: Chi-Square Test Statistics

	Never changed the operator
Chi-Square	199.856[a]
df	8
Asymp. Sig.	**.000**
a. 0 cells (0.0%) have expected frequencies less than 5. The minimum expected cell frequency is 27.8.	

Source: *Own findings*

SPSS gives several tests for significance and we will first focus on the Pearson Chi-Square test. This test begins by forming the Pearson test statistic which is asymptotically formed from the observed and expected cell counts. For each cell, the difference between the observed and expected counts is found or squared. This positive number is then divided by the expected count to account for different sizes of cells. Having constructed this value for each cell these are summed across all cells to give our test statistic which here is 199.856. This statistic follows a chi-squared distribution under the null hypothesis with a degree of freedom equal to 8. The statistics are then compared with the appropriate Chi-Squared distribution and this results in an asymptotic (2-sided) p-value which has a value of .000 (reported as p<.001). Here we see that the p-value is less than 0.05 and therefore we can reject the null hypothesis that the two variables are independent and there is therefore some relationship between the variables.

Null Hypothesis 3: Indian telecom sector is not affected by the disruptive innovation strategy *(Result: Null Hypothesis Rejected)*

Table 5.17a: Distinctive factors that caused disruption in the Indian telecom industry

	Strongly Agree	Agree	Neutral	Disagree	Strongly Disagree
Wide 4G Network	118	101	22	6	3
High-Speed Internet	105	105	31	6	3
Discounted and unlimited data tariff	90	99	45	10	6
Unlimited HD voice calls	89	106	46	7	2
Free apps subscription	68	101	50	23	8
Disruptive pricing strategy	75	95	57	18	5

Source: *Own findings*

Table 5.17a shows the respondents' agreement and disagreement on 5 points Likert scale where 1=Strongly Agree, 2= Agree, 3= Neutral, 4=Disagree, and 5=Strongly Disagree, and reveals that Indian telecom users strongly agree that the development, promotion, and adaptation of disruptive innovative technologies like wide network coverage, high-speed internet, unlimited data tariff and voice calls, free subscription of different applications, and pricing strategy affected the Indian telecom industry. These effects can also be clearly visible after the entrance of Reliance into the business.

Table 5.17b: One-Sample Test

	Test Value = 0				95% Confidence Interval of the Difference	
	t	df	Sig. (2-tailed)	Mean Difference	Lower	Upper
Wide 4G Connectivity	32.675	249	.000	1.70000	1.5975	1.8025
High-Speed Internet	33.649	249	.000	1.78800	1.6833	1.8927
Discounted and Unlimited Data Tariff	32.527	249	.000	1.97200	1.8526	2.0914
Unlimited HD voice calls	35.593	249	.000	1.90800	1.8024	2.0136
Free Apps subscription	33.453	249	.000	2.20800	2.0780	2.3380
Disruptive Pricing Strategy	34.009	249	.000	2.13200	2.0085	2.2555

Source: *Own findings*

In Table 5.17b one-sample test analysis also confirms the frequency analysis highlighted in Table 5.17a. Here, the Sig. value (2-tailed) is.000 (p<.001) for all the factors that caused disruption in the Indian telecom industry. So, null hypothesis is rejected.

Table 5.18a: At what level does each of the following service providers meet your overall expectations?

	Exceeded my expectations	Mostly met my expectations	Sometimes met my expectations	Rarely met my expectations
Reliance (Jio)	**73**	**111**	**46**	**20**
Vodafone Idea "Vi"	27	79	76	68
Airtel	50	95	65	40
BSNL	32	52	82	84

Source: *Own findings*

Table 5.18a reveals the Chi-Square descriptive of the user expectations in regard to the different service providers in the study area. It reveals that Reliance Jio meets the expectations of the users in comparison to the other telecom service providers. This also explains that the innovative disruptive technologies are successfully offered by Reliance Jio which understands the needs and demands of the users accordingly whereas other service providers are also trying to achieve the same objective by adapting and offering the same technologies. The chi-square test statistics in table 15b below reflect the same, the chi-square values are **72.656** for Reliance Jio and which is on the higher side, whereas Vodafone Idea "Vi"=27.920, Airtel=27.600, and BSNL=30.128 under the null hypothesis with a degree of freedom equal to 3 The statistics are then compared with the appropriate Chi-Squared distribution and this result in an asymptotic p-value which has a value of .000 (reported as p<.001). Here we see that the p-value is less than 0.05 and therefore we can reject the null hypothesis that the two variables are independent and there is therefore some relationship between the variables.

Table 5.18b: Chi-Square Test Statistics

	Reliance Jio	Vodafone Idea Vi	Airtel	BSNL
Chi-Square	**72.656ᵃ**	27.920ᵃ	27.600ᵃ	30.128ᵃ
df	3	3	3	3
Asymp. Sig.	.000	.000	.000	.000
a. 0 cells (.0%) have expected frequencies less than 5. The minimum expected cell frequency is 62.5.				

Source: *Own findings*

Null Hypothesis 4: There is no impact of disruption on the overall business of Jio Infocom Ltd. *(Result: Null Hypothesis Rejected)*

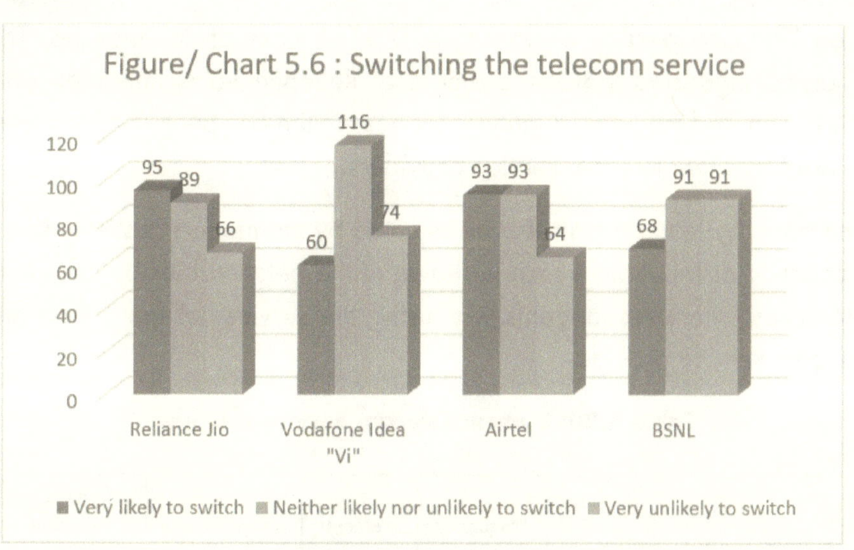

Source: *Own findings*

Above Figure/ Chart 5.6 reflects that maximum respondents using Jio telecom service were agreed **(95)** to switch the service provider if other competitor telecom industries will provide the better disruptive services. The chart also reflects that if BSNL adapts the new and innovative disruptive services and offering the same to the customers in the competitive prices BSNL will never **(91)** change the telecom service provider. The same statement can be proved by the chi-square analysis mentioned in the Table 16.

Table 5.19: Chi-Square Test Statistics

	Reliance Jio	Vodafone Idea Vi	Airtel	BSNL
Chi-Square	5.624[a]	20.384[a]	6.728[a]	4.232[a]
df	2	2	2	2
Asymp. Sig.	.060	.000	.035	.121
a. 0 cells (.0%) have expected frequencies less than 5. The minimum expected cell frequency is 83.3.				

Table 5.19 highlighted that the chi-square values of Reliance Jio **(5.624)**, Vodafone Idea "Vi" **(20.384)**, Airtel **(6.728)**, and BSNL **(4.232)** with the asymptotic p-value which has a value of .060, .000, .035, and .121 respectively. The p-value is less than 0.05 only in the case of Vodafone Idea "Vi" and p-value is more than 0.05 in case of Reliance Jio. This analysis suggested that the business of Reliance Jio is impacted after disruption and the same quality of services in the competitive prices were offered by other telecom service providers.

The same hypothesis can also be rejected by the mean statistics and the frequency distribution, which is shown in the below tables by excluding the cases where respondents was using the services of more than one telecom service provider:

Table 5.20: Current Telecom Service Provider

		Frequency	Percent	Valid Percent	Cumulative Percent
Valid	Airtel	35	14.0	14.0	14.0
	Reliance Jio	**99**	39.6	39.6	53.6
	Vodafone-Idea (Vi)	17	6.8	6.8	60.4
	BSNL/MTNL	4	1.6	1.6	62.0
	Other (More than one)	95	38.0	38.0	100.0
	Total	250	100.0	100.0	

Source: *Own findings*

Table 5.20 reflects the total number of respondents on the basis of their telecom service providers and revealed that the maximum numbers of users were using Reliance Jio. The table 5.21 below highlights the satisfaction level of the respondents in regard to their current service providers on 5-point Likert Scale where 1=Very satisfied, 2=Satisfied, 3=Neutral, 4=Dissatisfied, and 5=Very dissatisfied.

Table 5.21: Satisfaction level of the respondents

	Very Satisfied	Satisfied	Neutral	Dissatisfied	Very Dissatisfied	Mean
Satisfaction with the telecom executives	44	121	70	11	4	**2.24**
satisfaction with the sales department	30	114	83	17	6	**2.42**
Satisfaction with the network availability	42	113	58	26	11	**2.4**
Satisfaction with the VAS	26	102	91	26	5	**2.52**
Satisfaction with the internet facility	36	130	57	20	7	**2.32**
Satisfaction with the online services on website	35	129	67	16	3	**2.29**
Satisfaction with the current network vs. other network	42	141	46	14	7	**2.21**
Satisfaction with the network availability while traveling	23	104	67	47	9	**2.66**

Source: *Own findings*

Now after comparing the Chart 5.6 with the Table 5.21, we found that even after having satisfaction on the different parameters of the current telecom service provider, the maximum users from the total 250 respondents are from Reliance Jio **(see Table 5.20)** and they are ready to switch the telecom service if others will provide the better disruptive offers to them. This clearly revealed that the disruptive technologies have impacted the Reliance Jio business and we reject the Null Hypothesis on the basis of the data collected from different samples in the study area.

06

CONCLUSIONS, FINDINGS & SUGGESTIONS

Introduction

This chapter sets out the results of the questionnaire, initially assessing the descriptive statistics to establish the control variables and the basic characteristics of the disruptive technologies and telecom sector. This will be followed by an analysis of the remaining variables and aspects of the questionnaire under different headings. This will be followed by a critical discussion of the findings and their linkages to the existing literature and research in order to ascertain whether this new data supports or contradicts the existing information.

➢ Explaining "Disruptive Innovation," as it is that type of innovation that creates a new market and value network or enters at the bottom of an existing market and eventually displaces established market-leading firms, products, and alliances.

➢ The soul of Disruptive Innovation lies in transforms expensive or highly sophisticated products or services to more affordable and accessible to broader population. It involves the use of technologies to make them easy to use and available to the larger, non-targeted market.

➢ A disruptive company cares a lot about its customers and thinks that their needs, wants, and expectations are all in sync. In the process of meeting this loop of needs, wants, and expectations, these companies will create a new market.

➢ Evolutionary / Incremental / Sustaining Innovation is about continuous improvement of existing products or services to provide more value to an existing market, reducing defects and improving performance.

➢ Revolutionary / Discontinuous / Radical Innovation refers to the co-occurrence of a radical new mindset and radical new technology. These are new to the world or said game-changing innovations.

➢ Disruptive Innovation is eventually different from the Evolutionary and Revolutionary Innovation on the basis of degree of uses of new technology and degree of newness of the market.

➢ Disruptive technology is innovation in goods, services & business models which offer different alternatives and solutions to the market and are mostly aimed at non- traditional consumers. Disruptive Innovations has changed the way people live, work, and interact.

➢ In general, disruptive technology tries to bring full advantage and lower operating costs. It costs a lot of money to use disruptive technology because a lot of money goes into R&D, customising the technology, and training people to use it. Also, it takes time to build a strong, reliable framework when technology changes, like when a website or portal moves from the front line to the back end. In general, the way people of different ages interact with their bank to use digital services is different.

➢ Reliance Jio's advertising campaigns mainly focusing on the younger generation and getting good word of mouth publicity and hence got success.

➢ It has been observed that cost-effectiveness, free calls, no roaming charges, free channels, free caller tunes, and voice clarity were the main reasons for customers satisfaction. On the other hand, internet speed, compatibility with other SIM cards, and voice and video call connectivity were cited as reasons why customers were less satisfied.

➤ After the entry of Reliance Jio with affordable data pack with 4G connectivity and digital business model, disrupting so many industries and transforming them in the manner that they proliferated in a rapid manner like rapid growth of OTT platform like Netflix, Amazon Prime, Voot, Disney Hotsatar, Discovery+, MX Player etc. and other online platform like Spotify, Airbnb, Uber

➤ All the internet-based businesses and service platforms got the growing ecosystem due to easy and affordable availability of internet access. Such as Indian observed a sharp boom in video surfing after the launch of Jio and specifically in Covid-19 lockdown period.

➤ Apart from this Jio also affected badly the music tape, cassette and CD/DVD market as now peoples can easily avail the huge collection of songs on paid subscription based Gaana app at anytime and anywhere. They can enjoy these benefits while traveling, jogging, in peace time etc. Even Jio also gives free subscription of Jio Savan app which is parallelly a good music database in comparison to Gaana App.

➤ Disruptive Innovation is categorized as fast, unpredictable, messy and fatal in nature and it is beneficial to the business in the way as it improves the efficiency, sales of business, it also supports expansion of the market and startups.

➤ Tariff, Internet Speed, Service Quality, Branding, VAS, Goodwill of Operator, Creativity and Innovation are the key factors of customer migration towards Reliance Jio.

➤ At the introduction stage, Mobile Broadband, Jio Phone, LYF Smartphone and JioFi were the most popular products of the Jio. It also provides free subscription of more the 21 Jio Apps with the connection.

➢ Enabling technology, Innovative Business Model and Coherent Value Network are the key requirements for Disruptive Innovation.

➢ Reliance Jio has changed the face of the Indian telecom industry by changing the basis of service offering from being voice-based to a data-based platform.

➢ Reliance Jio in 2010 has bought 95% stake in *Infotel Broadband Services Limited (IBSL)* which was having 4G spectrum won during the auction. And after a 5 to 6 year of intense research and development of Indian consumers need, capability of telecom infrastructure, competitor's potential and government regulations and laws, they launched it in 2016.

➢ Reliance Jio after its launch in 2016, it acquired more than *50 million customers* in exactly 83 days with focus on giving India the power of the digital revolution, which means connecting everyone by giving the best connectivity at the best price.

➢ Reliance Jio has significantly increased the accessibility and affordability of data. Just by offering cheap data prices it compelled the most conservative customers even to use the internet and so as per a study conducted by Institute of Competitiveness it also led the consumers to annual financial savings of approx. Rs 60,000 crores.

➢ Average prices per GB of 3G data have dropped from Rs 250 to Rs 10. Such a drastic reduction in data prices has not only brought the internet within the reach of larger proportion of the Indian population but has also allowed newer segments of society to use and experience it for the first time.

➢ Due to improved accessibility and affordability of data our country became the highest mobile data user all over the world within a span of just six months since the launch of Jio.

➢ In order to address multiple socio-economic needs of the customers, the company has attempted to create a digital platform offering

- applications ranging from health, education, banking, entertainment and so on.

➤ Econometric analysis of Institute of Competitiveness report shows, entry of Reliance Jio with widespread digital network would boost India's GDP by about 5.65 percent, if everything else in the economy remains constant.

➤ It has been identified that the new market creation, value addition, reduction of complexities, support of startups, updating technologies, India's IT market, online transportation and lodging services are the leading opportunities to disruptive innovation apart from this music and video streaming, Inter platform instant messaging apps, cryptocurrencies, Augmented Reality, Online education, Cable TV Network, selling network equipment's, SMS marketing, Artificial Intelligence, Machine Learning, Internet of Things are the innovative developments in the Indian technological market and it open a broad opportunity for Disruptive Innovation in India.

➤ Various issues have also been observed like Impatient leadership, lack of innovation ecosystem and culture, resistance to change, inadequate benchmarking, ethical issues, adaptability, untested & time consuming, network coverage and internet speed, buggy in Jio apps, fast drain out of battery of phone and VOLTE support on old phone.

➤ Still after the great success of Reliance Jio there are some big challenges to them like adaptability, competition, market acceptance, sustainability, changing government policies, compliance and legal violations, data security & privacy, ethical and legal concerns, fake chatbot, complexities in the IoT.

➤ It is found that telecommunication market is much dynamic and volatile in respect of technology upgradation like 1G (analog) after introduction in 1979, got rigorous updation in respect of its network standards, access technologies but soon 2G has launched in early 1990s' to overcome the issues in 1G and so 2G was the first generation of digital radio technologies working on four standards, namely GSM, CDMA, Interim Standard and PDC which further evolved into GPRS (pre-3G radio technology), EDGE to provide better digital services to the customers. Ever-growing needs of subscribers and technological advancement has led the market to move to the 3G technology which focused on the improvement of voice services with the aim of offering high-speed data and multimedia connectivity to subscribers. They are supporting speed of 144 kbps to greater than 2 Mbps. 3G uses the network standard UMTS or W-CDMA with further number of upgradations as HSDPA and HSUPA this 3G network has been evolved. This 3G has now been evolved as 4G launched in 2016 in India. The UMTS has now been upgraded to LTE which is also sometimes called 3.9G or Super 3G. With the potency of speed of 200 Mbps this LTE further VOLTE is presently administering the Indian Telecom Market. Further 5G has been launched and labelled as 'ultra-fast, ultra-reliable, ultra-high capacity transmitting with 1 Gbps speed and capability of 100 billion connections of Internet of Things. 5G is the future of telecommunication market.

➢ It has been observed that Pre Jio there was 10 telecom companies operating the Indian telecom market, where Airtel have the maximum market share of 24.8% followed by Vodafone 19.1%, Idea 17% BSNL 9.3%, Aircel 8.6% and 5 others 21.2.

➢ In the starting phase Reliance Jio consumers faced voice connectivity problem to other network and other competitors raised the voice to authorities against the Jio about its 'Predatory Pricing' and free voice calls which was the source of 75 to 77% of total revenue for them. So, they said they weren't mandated by law to connect to Reliance Jio, However, after TRAI refusal to mediate in this, all companies added more points of interconnection for Reliance Jio.

➢ Reliance Jio strategized its launched in a way as many people got a free SIM card, or maybe even a cheap phone, they could use the services as long as they were free. If these users have a good experience, they may switch to paid services in the future.

➢ After launch of Reliance Jio only 4 market players left in the market and according to a report by TRAI from September 2020, Reliance Jio had the most subscribers with 35% of the market. Airtel and Vodafone-Idea (Vi) were next with 29% and 26%, respectively. As a public company, BSNL was able to stay in business and now has a 10% market share only.

➢ Reliance Jio added a huge 4.22 million wireless customers in June 2022 in comparison to Airtel having only 0.79 million. The number of low-paying customers of Jio has gone down while the number of smartphone users has gone up. This is mostly because of the *low-cost Jio Phone Next* smart phones.

➢ It has been recorded that Vodafone Idea (Vi) and BSNL lost about 1.8 million and 1 million customers respectively in June 2022 due to trouble with 4G operations.

➢ However, it is also recorded as, Bharti Airtel has the most active subscribers, at around 98.41%. This means that of all the people who have signed up for its service, close to 98% are actually using it, while Reliance Jio has only 92.79%. Also, 85.2% of Vodafone-Idea's customers were still using the service.

➢ In terms of market share of total wireless subscribers upto June 2022, Jio comfortably leads with a 36% market share. Airtel's market share improved slightly to reach 31.63%, while Vi's market share decreased to 22.37%. In all, private telecom players accounted for 90% of the market share in India's telecom industry in June 2022.

➢ When it comes to the overall share of the market including (Wired and Wireless), Reliance Jio is again the leader with a huge 52.33 percent share. Bharti Airtel comes in second with a 27.39% share.

Vodafone Idea had 15.35 percent of the market, and BSNL came in second with 3.12 percent.

➢ Ultra-cheap data, Increased consumption of online content, Free voice calls, Growth of 4G smartphones, Faster, mobile data, record user acquisition, Improved broadband Internet availability, Ease to online streaming services are the post disruption change in values & benefits being offered in Indian telecom market.

➢ Reliance Jio announced fibre-to-the-home service in September 2019, which includes home broadband, cable television, and phone services. For that, Reliance Industries has raised Rs.1.65 lakh crore (US$22 billion) by selling nearly one third of its stock investment in Reliance Jio Platforms as of September 2020.

➢ Reliance Jio adopted AARRR strategy to disrupt the Indian telecom market i.e. Acquisition, Activation, Retention, Referral and Revenue. This is some time said as 2A and 3R strategy. It used penetration pricing strategy to reap all the market opportunities and add more and more customer base.

➢ Reliance Jio for market penetration also adopted digital marketing in aggressive manner and also used many social media platforms to run the promotional campaign. On Instagram alone, it has more than 960k followers, has a strong presence on YouTube, with more than 2.36 million subscribers, on Facebook, where more than 2.5 million people follow it and even more than 666k follower on Twitter. Few digital campaigns were very popular named Digital India, Home Delivered, Jio Cheers Cricket and Jio Cricket Play-Along and so on.

➢ Some of the Reliance Jio marketing campaign was very sensitive as they encourage Indian heritage in their social media messaging, touching indigenous emotions of customers through *Humara India* and *#VocalForLocal* culture.

➢ Bridging the gap between merchants and their customers. Jio's plan is a one-of-a-kind way to get into any business that uses technology.

Some specific industries are Education, Health Care, Media, and many others.

➤ In the SWOT analysis of Reliance Jio various opportunities and threat has been identified and measures has been suggested to convert them into opportunities and strength.

Descriptive Statistical findings

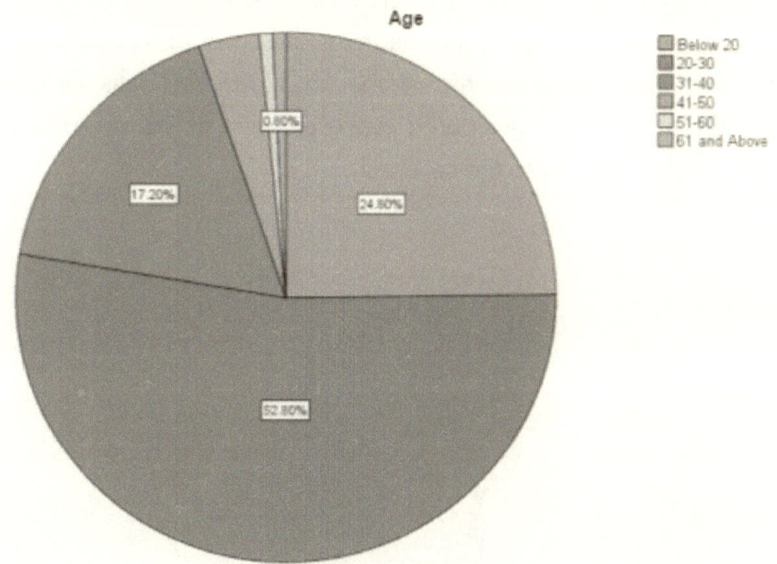

Chart 6.1: Age
Source: *Own findings*

➤ **Age:** As it is socially apparent that telecom industry and different disruptive technologies offered by the industry have far greater appeal to the younger generation. This study sought to target people from all age groups to understand the role of disruptive innovation technology and Indian telecom industry. The age distribution of the research population is shown in chart 6.1 below:

As can be seen from the above, **52.80%** of the research populations are between the ages of 20 to 30, which would suggest that this is the clear target market to understand the role of disruptive technologies in the Indian telecom industry.

> **Educational Qualifications:** This demographic is useful to understand the relationship between innovative disruptive technologies and level of education. The results of this element are shown in chart 6.2 overleaf. As can be seen from the chart 6.2, by far the greatest proportion of the research population have either a degree or a post graduate degree **(38.80%),** this is also aligned with the average age distribution of the research population and the expected demographic of the location. This tells us that the population can be considered representative of the area, and thus adds further weight to the research.

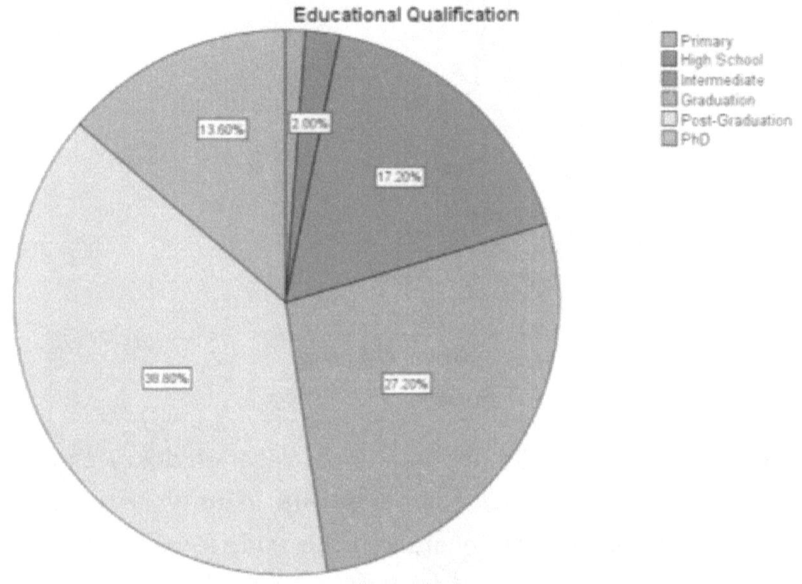

Chart 6.2: Educational Qualifications
Source: *Own findings*

> **Occupation Status:** Chart 6.3 below represents the occupation status of the research population, and reveals that maximum

population are either student **(48.80%)** or employed in different sectors **(38.40%).** The demographic analysis in chart 6.3 highlights that the students and employed users of the Indian telecom industry are very much interested in different innovative disruptive technologies offered by the service provider.

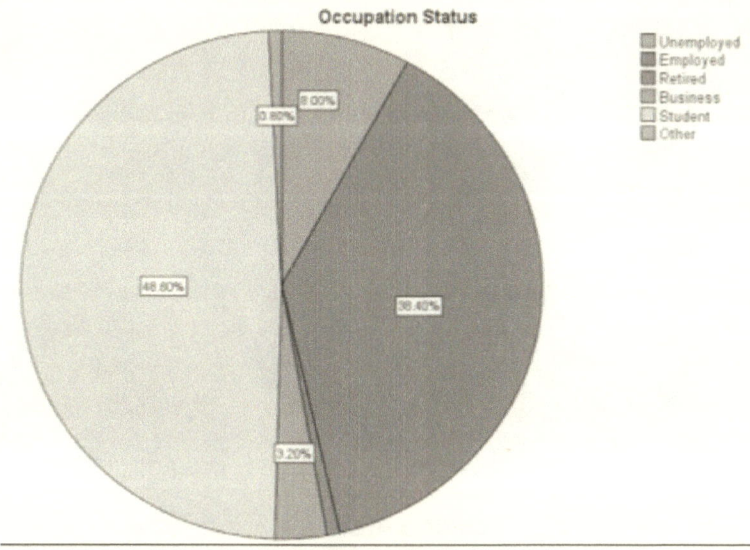

Chart 6.3: Occupation Status
Source: *Own findings*

> **Locality:** Demographic analysis of the locality in the Chart 6.4 reflects that the greater populations in the selected research area are from urban background **(65.20%).** It also reveals the significant relationship between the research population from urban area and the understanding of the need of the research problem. It is clear from the analysis in the chart that telecom users from the urban area have better understanding about the disruptive technologies and different innovative offers provided by the Indian telecom service providers on the basis of such technologies.

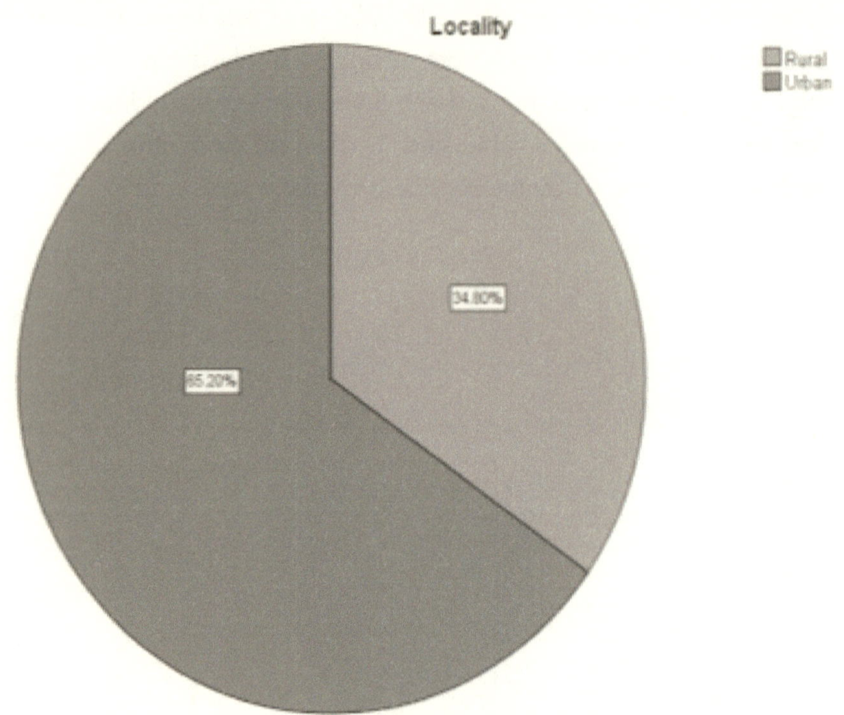

Chart 6.4: Locality
Source: *Own findings*

> **Hypothesis Statistical Analysis:** This section of the research is devoted to setting out the results of the statistical analysis under the three quantitative hypothesis i.e., First, Disruptive innovation has no effect on new market and new product or services, Second, Indian Telecom Sector is not affected by Disruptive Innovation Strategy, and Third, There is no impact of disruption on overall business of Jio Infocom Ltd. The questionnaire was analyzed using a combination of SPSS and Excel to provide frequency analysis, correlation, chi-square, and other statistical methods which help to explain the relationships between the variables examined in the study. It should be noted at the outset of this study that the research population of 250 can be considered sufficiently large for the responses to have statistical meaning and validity under the analysis carried out.

Null Hypothesis: Disruptive innovation has no effect on new market and new product or services.

As seen from the responses, a highly significant i.e., **99** respondents use Reliance Jio and indicating that this is an ideal service provider for communicating with a young target audience or market segment. Not only does this finding correspondent with anecdotal evidence on the extent of Reliance Jio use, but also indicates that users are highly satisfied with the services offered by the company. On the basis of the analysis it can be noted that the maximum users are not willing to change the current service provider because the company is offering more innovative disruptive technologies to the users from the beginning in comparison to the other service providers. Whereas, other service providers are now also trying to adapt and offer more disruptive innovative technologies as same as Reliance Jio to be in the competition in the continuously growing new market and the demand of new product or services. The observed p-value **(.000; p<.0.05)** from chi-square analysis to test the null hypothesis also revealed that disruptive innovation in the telecom industry mark its effect, therefore, we reject the null hypothesis.

Null Hypothesis: Indian Telecom Sector is not affected by Disruptive Innovation Strategy

To test the above-mentioned hypothesis 5-points Likert's scale method was used to observe the respondent attitude on the factors that caused disruption in the Indian telecom industry and affected the whole market especially after the entry of Reliance Jio in the competition. The chart below shows that maximum research population where strongly agree that disruptive innovative technologies affected the Indian telecom sector.

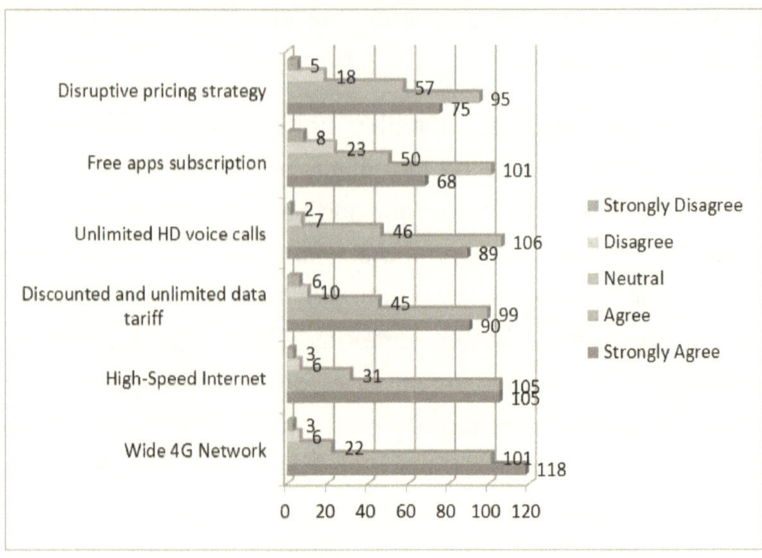

Chart 6.5: Factors causing disruption
Source: *Own Findings*

The same can be proved by One-Sample Test analysis where recorded p-value **(.000)** is less than **(.001)**. The null hypothesis was rejected also in the Chi-Square analysis where again recorded p-value was **.000** and less than **0.05**. The analysis to test this null hypothesis here also highlighted that Reliance Jio services were met the expectations of the respondents in an exceeded manner.

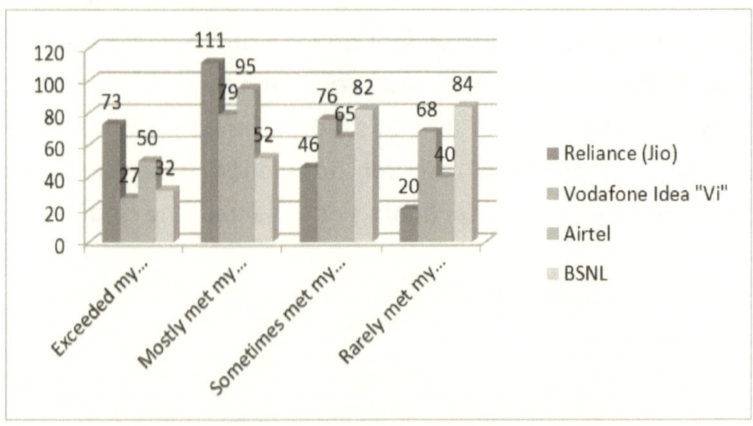

Chart 6.6: Expectations of the Respondents
Source: *Own findings*

Null Hypothesis: There is no impact of disruption on overall business of Jio Infocom Ltd

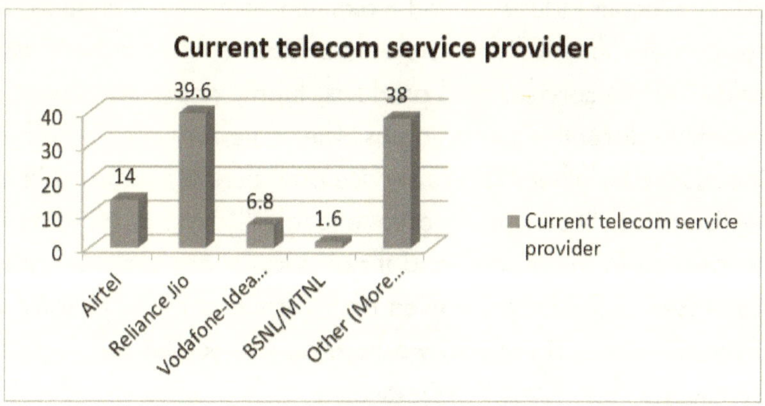

Chart 6.7: Current telecom service provider
Source: *Own findings*

To test the last null hypothesis frequency analysis in the chart reveals that 39.6% of the research population was using Reliance Jio, and the below chart reflects the satisfaction level of the research population in regards to the services offered by their current telecom service provider. The frequency analysis in the below chart showed that maximum respondents are satisfied with the services offered by their current telecom service provider.

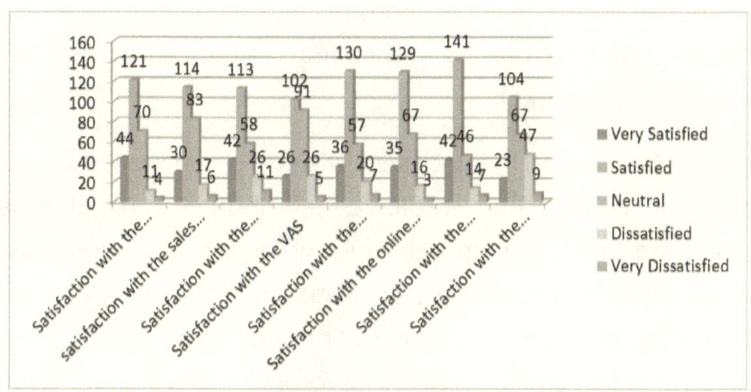

Chart 6.8: Satisfaction Level of Customer
Source: *Own findings*

The above analysis clearly mentioned that disruptive innovative technologies have been made the major effect on the telecom industry. The Indian telecom industry noted maximum competitive changes in the services offered once Reliance Jio enters into the telecom business with new and effective services and products, highly designed according to the innovative disruptive technologies. The same services and offers are now introduced by other telecom service providers to their users in highly competitive prices like Airtel, Vodafone Idea "Vi", and BSNL to maintain the competition in the market and these adaptations are now affecting the businesses of Reliance Jio even after receiving the high satisfaction level from his users. Therefore, we here also reject the null hypothesis, and concluded that disruptive innovative technologies are developing new market for the users of each age group, locality, and economic class and all the Indian telecom service providers are trying to capture the market as per the need and demand of the customers.

CONCLUSION

Taking into account the foregoing discussions and analysis in respect of the disruptive innovation technologies in Indian telecom industry, as determined in both primary and secondary study and research, has led to the following conclusions. These changes can apply both to the users and industry who are hoping to harness the disruptive innovation technologies on Indian telecom industry as a means of increasing their brand awareness and directly promoting their products and offers to their desired target market.

Conceptual background behind the "Disruptive Innovation," is as it is that type of innovation that creates a new market and value network or enters at the bottom of an existing market and eventually displaces established market-leading firms, products, and alliances. Its theme lies in transforming expensive or highly sophisticated products or services to more affordable and accessible to broader population. It involves the use of technologies to make them easy to use and available to the larger, non-targeted market. As far as Revolutionary and Evolutionary

Innovation is concern the Disruptive Innovation is eventually different from them on the basis of degree of uses of new technology and degree of newness of the market.

This research identified that in 2010 after acquiring the 95% stake in *Infotel Broadband Services Limited (IBSL)* which was having 4G spectrum won during the auction Reliance Jio has changed the face of the Indian telecom industry by changing the basis of service offering from being voice-based to a data-based platform. After its launch in 2016, it acquired more than *50 million customers* in exactly 83 days which was a record in itself in the history of telecom sector. Various disruptive factors have also been identified governing customer satisfaction such as affordable and disruptive pricing strategy, free apps subscription, unlimited HD voice calls, unlimited and discounted data tariff, high speed internet, wide 4G network, and Reliance Jio got the maximum no of count by the respondents in comparison to its competitors. Due to affordable and unlimited data offering by Reliance Jio Indian became the highest mobile data user all over the world within a span of just six months since the launch of Jio. Eventually, it has also given a shining to the India's digital economy. Rapid growth of various OTT platform, digital public services and other online business are the evidence of it. Reliance Jio disruption has also affected many other businesses such as cassette and CD/DVD market replaced by various online apps. Even Reliance Jio offers free subscription of its 21 Jio Apps, many of which are badly affecting the other market/ business such as newspaper/ magazine, Live TV with all channel, cinema, cloud storage, security, video conferencing, e-commerce market etc. It has also been identified that Reliance Jio is still having huge opportunities in the Indian telecom market while it must keep its eye on prevailing issues and have quick resolution of it. Still it has many challenges to deal with like dynamic market, sustainability, ethical and legal issues etc. This research also talks about generation growth of telecom technology in India.

In India, Jio has become a successful brand, and their main goal is to make sure their customers are happy. It gives free calls, data services, and SMS services. The free introductory offer from Reliance Jio changed a lot the consumer behaviour and competitor's business orientation. It affected the balance of the telecom industry, and many of the competitors in Indian mobile network providers resorted to merger and acquisition. Most of the respondents cum users of Jio who took part in the study were satisfied with Jio's services, and they told the company that it should improve its network coverage and overcome the calling congestion problem. Reliance Jio is getting a bigger share of the Indian market every day. It can be said that the company will do well in the telecom business in the near future.

The Reliance Jio growth will depend on how consumers react to the prices. As it has already been said in this study about price-sensitive customers, they want to get the most out of the least amount of money they spend. The study shows the new strategy that Jio is using to deal with problems. In the past, Reliance Communication lost their market, but now when the Reliance Jio has entered the market, the situation has changed. But there will always be competition between mobile operators. The one who goes above and beyond what the customer wants will be the king of the market always.

The research demonstrated that there is a direct relationship between age and telecom services as younger people were more influenced than older people. This information is useful as it helps telecom industries directly target their desired market, and through the existence of known disruptive innovative technologies can directly attract the new customers. Most of the respondents are students or employed having PG or UG degree, belonging to urban area shows that telecom users have better understanding about the disruptive technologies and different innovative offers provided by the Indian telecom service providers on the basis of such technologies and gain maximum advantage of it. Jio announced fibre-to-the-home service in 2019 for home broadband, cable television, and phone services and on account of this it raised Rs 1.65 lakh crore by selling its one third stake. Reliance Jio adopted AARRR strategy and penetration pricing strategy to reap all the market opportunities and add more and more customer base. As Reliance Jio has a strong presence and followers on various digital/ social media platforms, So, it adopted digital marketing in aggressive manner and also used many social media platforms to run the promotional campaign. This research is devoted with one qualitative null hypothesis i.e. Disruptive Innovation Strategy has no difference from Evolutionary and Revolutionary Innovation Strategy and three quantitative null hypothesis i.e., First, Disruptive innovation has no effect on new market and new product or services, Second, Indian Telecom Sector is not affected by Disruptive Innovation Strategy, and Third, There is no impact of disruption on overall business of Jio Infocomm Ltd. All the four hypothesis has been rejected in the data analysis. That means, Indian telecom industry noted maximum competitive changes in the services offered once Reliance Jio enters into the telecom business with new and effective services and products, highly designed according to the innovative disruptive technologies. The same services and offers are now introduced by other telecom service providers to their users in highly competitive prices like Airtel, Vodafone Idea "Vi", and BSNL to maintain the competition in the market and these adaptations are now affecting the businesses of Reliance Jio even after receiving the high satisfaction level from his users.

SUGGESTIONS

> As telecom industry have been shown to have a direct influence on the users' decision-making process, specifically at the precise point of determining whose products to purchase and to encourage users to co-create in building the brand of a product, it is strongly advices that telecom industry develop and actively promote innovative disruptive technologies enabled products and services in order to raise awareness.

> The research has demonstrated that the majority of users influenced by new technologies and competitive strategies. Therefore, there may be some benefit in incentivizing users to leave positive features offered by the service providers.

➤ The research also demonstrates that there is a stronger incentive for users to believe the competitive strategies; therefore, industry should possibly consider setting up different or linked products and services for different nations.

➤ Reliance Jio is offering its 4G services to the rural areas also but should work on the network connectivity and speed to satisfy the rural customers. They should also work on technical awareness to the rural customers.

➤ Telecom operators should focus on network availability and affordable pricing to reach to the maximum no of subscriber.

➤ Call drop and call inter connection issues is one of the most problematic issue which should be considered by the telecom companies for technological upgradation.

➤ Mostly it's the network coverage and predatory pricing during the initial months after the launch of Reliance Jio that got them such huge market share. This disruption is not limited to telecom industry only rather it has affected the whole economy in a very complex way which certainly are disruptive in nature. The normative positions of such disruption is an issue of serious academic enquiry. So, it is the research scope for further investigation.

➤ Telecom operators should focus on improvement of network coverage and quality of service if they want to expand their customer base and pricing aspect of tariff which are increasing frequent.

➤ Telecom companies should make a proper strategy for price rising with number of validity days, In 2021, December Telecom Industry raised price, in which Reliance jio also hiked their price with 21% but they also reduced validity days of recharge plans. Its only my suggestion for research point of view focused on both these terms for sustainable development in Indian Telecom Industry.

➢ Resolution of complaints should be as early as possible so that it will not create any problem to the customer. Customer oriented service and flexible tariff rates are to be recommended for the good customer friendly services. Also, there must be transparency in their services, polices, programs.

➢ Proper testing, research and development should be done prior launch of 5G that it should not incur loss to humans, animals and the environment.

➢ The reliance Jio should revise the monthly packages so that economically backward peoples of the society can use them easily. Preferably, the school going children who are attending classes online should less burdened with extra amount including both school and internet fees.

➢ Company need to focus on the plans that can be affordable for middle- and lower-class peoples as well as the students, as higher prices sometimes lead to dissatisfaction.

➢ Reliance should get a strong foothold in the market by moving into rural and remote areas of the country that haven't been touched yet. They should do this by putting ads in local mail, hat bazaars, TV projectors, and other places.

➢ After the entry of Jio in the market peoples are more habitual towards free offers, discounts and rewards that actually is not the strong factor to build brand loyalty and certainly the customer migrates to the other service provider if it gets a discounted good plan. So, the company should make strategies to increase the brand loyalty in the customers.

➢ They should work on maximum consumer inclusion rather focusing only premium consumers. They should also work on technical awareness to the rural customers through awareness campaign. Jio should revise the monthly packages so that economically weaker section of the society can use them easily.

➢ Reliance Jio disruption has affected the whole economy in a very complex way and initiated the digital revolution. So, it should be handled with very care otherwise it will become worst for the economy. Rapid growth of OTT platform, online payment and other online platform / business are the factors for the growth of digital economy.

➢ Disruptions can have negative consequences for individuals and industries who cannot adapt to the changes. eg. digital photography has led to the decline of the traditional photography industry. This has resulted in layoffs and the closure of photo labs across the country. Reliance Jio and other operators can organize social issues awareness campaign through its digital platforms. Companies should carefully integrate the future technologies such as 'Internet of Things', Artificial Intelligence (AI) and Machine Learning (ML) with social need and demand for its growth.

REFERNCES

1. Hough, C. (2020, March 23). *Different Types of Innovation in Business: Why One Size Doesn't Fit All.* Idea Drop | Idea Management Software. Retrieved April 2, 2022, from https://ideadrop.co/innovation-management/different-types-of-innovation/

2. Vandenberg, S. (2021, December 21). *How Do You Define Innovation and Make It Practical and Saleable to Senior Management?* Innovation Management. Retrieved August 6, 2022, from https://innovationmanagement.se/2008/01/07/how-do-you-define-innovation-and-make-it-practical-and-saleable-to-senior-management/

3. Alcor Fund. (2021, August 14). *The Innovation Process: Importance, Steps, Types, Examples, and Risks Involved.* Retrieved August 6, 2022, from https://alcorfund.com/insight/the-innovation-process-importance-steps-types-examples-and-risks-involved/

4. *Disruptive Innovation Definition.* (2022, March 23). Investopedia. Retrieved August 6, 2022, from https://www.investopedia.com/terms/d/disruptive-innovation.asp

5. Urbinati, A., Chiaroni, D., Chiesa, V., Franzò, S., & Frattini, F. (2018, May 14). An Exploratory Analysis on the Contextual Factors that Influence Disruptive Innovation: The Case of Uber. *International Journal of Innovation and Technology*

Management, 15(03), 1850024. https://doi.org/10.1142/s0219877018500244

6. Huang, S. (2021, October 8). *Five Characteristics of Disruption All Leaders Must Know*. https://www.linkedin.com/pulse/five-characteristics-disruption-all-leaders-must-know-sean-huang

7. Wikipedia contributors. (2022, September 11). *Disruptive innovation*. Wikipedia. https://en.wikipedia.org/wiki/Disruptive_innovation

8. Ahmad, M. (2022, January 28). *Full Guide on Disruptive Innovation – Benefits, Examples, and Implementation*. TetraNoodle.com. https://tetranoodle.com/disruptive-innovation/

9. *Disruptive Innovation: Definition, Examples & Advantages*. (2021, May 5). MIT ID INNOVATION. https://mitidinnovation.com/recreation/disruptive-innovation-definition-examples-advantages/#:%7E:text=Disruptive%20innovation%20modifies%20how%20a,benefits%20the%20company%20a%20lot.

10. SYDLE. (n.d.). *Post title*. https://www.sydle.com/blog/types-of-innovation-619541bf351e93287c42a7de/

11. Allan, AJ, Randy, LJ, 2005, Writing the Winning Thesis or Dissertation. A Step-by-Step Guide, Corwin Press, California

12. Brown RB, 2006, Doing Your Dissertation in Business and Management: The Reality of Research and Writing, Sage Publications

13. Cohen, L, Manion, L, Morrison, K & Morrison, RB, 2007, Research Methods in Education, Routledge

14. O'Leary Z. 2004 "The essential guide to doing research". Sage.

15. *Population Definition in Statistics and How to Measure It*. (2022, July 14).

16. Investopedia. Retrieved August 16, 2022, from https://www.investopedia.com/terms/p/population.asp

17. Rosaroso, R. C. (2015, June). Using reliability measures in test validation. *European Scientific Journal, 11*(8), 369–377.

18. Middleton, F. (2022, August 31). *Reliability vs. Validity in Research | Difference, Types and Examples*. Scribbr. Retrieved September 16, 2022, from https://www.scribbr.com/methodology/reliability-vs-validity/

19. Ghauri, P. & Gronhaug, K. (2005). Research Methods in Business Studies, Harlow, FT/Prentice Hall

20. F. Dieffenbacher, S. (2022, September 1). Different Types of Innovation & How to Choose your Innovation Goal? Digital Leadership. Retrieved August 18, 2022, from https://digitalleadership.com/blog/types-of-innovation/

21. Ringberg, T., Reihlen, M., & Rydén, P. (2019). The technology-mindset interactions: Leading to incremental, radical or revolutionary innovations. Industrial Marketing Management, 79, 102–113. https://doi.org/10.1016/j.indmarman.2018.06.009

22. Leyes, K. (2020, May 19). *The Importance Of Innovating Disruptively In Business*. Forbes. Retrieved August 18, 2022, from https://www.forbes.com/sites/forbesbusinesscouncil/2020/05/19/the-importance-of-innovating-disruptively-in-business/?sh=7e6a1cc757e2

23. Mckinney, P. (2022, February 4). *Disruptive Innovation: The Theory Behind How It Works and Its Impact on Society*. Phil McKinney - Innovation Mentor and Coach. Retrieved August 18, 2022, from https://philmckinney.com/disruptive-innovation-the-theory-behind-how-it-works-and-its-impact-on-society/

24. Wikipedia contributors. (2022b, August 13). Jio. Wikipedia. Retrieved September 19, 2022, from https://en.wikipedia.org/wiki/Jio

25. Twin, A. (2022, March 23). *Disruptive Innovation*. Investopedia. Retrieved May 2, 2022, from https://www.investopedia.com/terms/d/disruptive-innovation.asp

26. Dr. M. A. Sikandar, Dr. M. A. S. (2019). *Age of Disruptive Innovation Through Digital Technologies in India, Issues, Challenges and Opportunities. International Journal of Human Resource Management and Research, 9(3), 175–180. https://doi.org/10.24247/ijhrmrjun201921.*

27. Wikipedia contributors. (2022, June 11). *Disruptive innovation*. Wikipedia. Retrieved July 3, 2022, from https://en.wikipedia.org/wiki/Disruptive_innovation#:%7E:text=to%20its%20competitor%22.,Theory,the%20%22technology%20mudslide%20hypothesis%22.

28. Petzold, N., Landinez, L., & Baaken, T. (2019). Disruptive innovation from a process view: A systematic literature review. *Creativity and Innovation Management, 28*(2), 157–174. https://doi.org/10.1111/caim.12313.

29. Danneels, Erwin (2004). Disruptive Technology Reconsidered: A Critique and Research Agenda. *Journal of Product Innovation Management* 21(4):246–258.

30. Christensen, Clayton M. (1997). *The Innovator's Dilemma: When New Technologies Cause Great Firms to Fail.* Boston: Harvard Business School Press.

31. Christensen, Clayton M. and Raynor, Michael (2003). *The Innovator's Solution: Creating and Sustaining Successful Growth.* Boston: Harvard Business School Press.

32. Henderson, Rebecca and Clark, Kim (1990). Architectural Innovation: The Reconfiguration of Existing Product Technologies and the Failure of Established Firms. *Administrative Science Quarterly* 35:9–30.

33. Markides, Constantinos and Geroski, Paul (2005). *Fast Second: How Smart Companies Bypass Radical Innovation to Enter and Dominate New Markets*. San Francisco: Jossey-Bass.

34. Charitou, Constantinos and Markides, Constantinos (2003). Responses to Disruptive Strategic Innovation. *Sloan Management Review* 44(2):55–63.

35. Baatartogtokh, B., & King, A. A. (2015). How Useful Is the Theory of Disruptive Innovation? *MIT Sloan Management Review, 57*(1), 77–90. http://mitsmr.com/1LezH2O

36. Tushman, M.L. and Anderson, P. (1986) Technological discontinuities and organizational environments. *Administrative Science Quarterly* 31, 439-465.

37. Tushman, M.L. and Nadler, D. (1986) Organizing for innovation. *California Management Review* 74-92.

38. Veryzer, R.W. (1998) Discontinuous Innovation and the New Product Development Process. *Journal of Product Innovation Management*, (15), 304-321.

39. Hamel, G. (2000) *Leading the Revolution*, Harvard Business School Press, Boston, Massachusetts.

40. Thomond, P., & Lettice, F. (2002). Disruptive Innovation Explored. *Engineering Conference, July.* http://www.insightcentre.com/resources/DIExplored-CEConf2002final.pdf

41. Assink, M. (2006), "Inhibitors of disruptive innovation capability: a conceptual model", *European Journal of Innovation Management*, Vol. 9 No. 2, pp. 215-233. https://doi.org/10.1108/14601060610663587

42. Młodawski, W. (2019). *Cutting-Edge Business Models in The Age of Digital Disruption -Examples, Prospects, and Key Economic and Legal Challenges* [PhD Thesis].

43. Urbinati, A., Chiaroni, D., Chiesa, V., Franzò, S., & Frattini, F. (2019). How Incumbents Manage Waves of Disruptive

Innovations: An Exploratory Analysis of the Global Music Industry. *International Journal of Innovation and Technology Management*, *16*(1). https://doi.org/10.1142/S0219877019500068

44. Travica, B. (Ed.). (2019). Informing View of Organization: Strategic Perspective: Strategic Perspective. IGI Global.

45. Guo, J., Pan, J., Guo, J., Gu, F., & Kuusisto, J. (2019). Measurement framework for assessing disruptive innovations. Technological Forecasting and Social Change, 139, 250-265.

46. Chatterjee, B. (2017). "Disruptive Innovation and Reliance Jio – A Descriptive Study" . *International Journal of Research Culture Society* , 1

47. Christensen, C. M., McDonald, R., Altman, E. J., & Palmer, J. E. (2018). Disruptive Innovation: An Intellectual History and Directions for Future Research. *Journal of Management Studies*, 55, 1043-1078. https://doi.org/10.1111/joms.12349.

48. Michael E. Raynor, R. G. (2011). "Disruptive innovation: the Southwest Airlines case revisited", Strategy & Leadership. Advances in Economics and Business Management (AEBM) p-ISSN: 2394-1545.

49. Russell, C. L. (2018). 5 G wireless telecommunications expansion: Public health and environmental implications. *Environmental Research*, *165*, 484–495. https://doi.org/10.1016/j.envres.2018.01.016.

50. Joy, T., and Bahl, S. (2018), "Disruption by reliance jio in telecom industry", *International Journal of Pure and Applied Mathematics*, Vol. 118 No. 20, pp. 43-49.

51. Roy, R., & Islam, M. (2017). Nuanced role of relevant prior experience: sales takeoff of disruptive products and product innovation with disrupted technology in industrial robotics. In *Entrepreneurship, Innovation, and Platforms*. Emerald Publishing Limited.

52. Yadav, N., & Gupta, K. (2020). Disruptive innovation in saturated Indian telecom space: a case of Reliance Jio. *International Journal of Business Innovation and Research, 23*(1), 127-140.

53. Vialle, P., Whalley, J., Curwen, P., & Parisot, X. (2020). Disruption in mobile industries: Free Mobile and Reliance Jio. In *ISPIM Conference Proceedings* (pp. 1-12). The International Society for Professional Innovation Management (ISPIM).

54. Mukhopadhyay, S., Whalley, J. (2021) The emergence and evolution of a disruptive platform ecosystem: evidence from the Indian mobile services industry. *Electron Markets* . https://doi.org/10.1007/s12525-021-00495-y

55. Ahluwalia, S., Mahto, R. V., & Walsh, S. T. (2017). Innovation in small firms: Does family vs. non-family matter?. *Journal of Small Business Strategy, 27*(3), 39-49.

56. Madhavan, P. M., & Chirputkar, A. (2020). Analysis of the Impact of Reliance Jio Infocomm Ltd on Indian Economy: a Case Study. *Pjaee, 17*(6), 4452–4461.

57. McClellan, S., Low, S., & Tan, W. T. (2004). Disruptive technologies and their affect on global telecommunications. *Advances in Computers*, 61, 199-273.

58. Yu, D., & Hang, C. C. (2010). A reflective review of disruptive innovation theory. *International journal of management reviews*, 12(4), 435-452.

59. Latzer, M. (2009). Information and communication technology innovations: radical and disruptive?. *New Media & Society*, 11(4), 599-619

60. Upreti, H., Malhotra, R. K., Ojha, M. K., Garg, A., & Pant, K. (2020). Customer Satisfaction from Service Aspects of Reliance Jio: A Comparative Study for Pre and Post Price Hike Period. *International Journal of Management, 11*(08).

61. Boobalan, C. and Jayaraman, K. (2017) Customers' satisfaction towards Reliance Jio sim with special reference to Dharmapuri district, *ICTACT journal on management studies*, 03(3), 547-552.

62. Brahmani, N. and Vamsi, S., (2017) Customer satisfaction towards Reliance Jio: An Empirical study. *IISTEM International conference*, 28-30.

63. Chinthala, G. Madhurim, X. H. and Kumar, K., (2017) Customer Satisfaction Towards Telecommunication Service Provider – A Study on Reliance JIO, *International Journal of Engineering and Management Research*, 7(2), 398-402.

64. Daga, T. Chandra, V. and Malik, A. (2018) Effect of Reliance Jio on Digital India, *International Journal of Advance Research*, 6(6), 395-441.

65. Gupta, A. Raghav, K and Dhakad, P, (2019) The Effect on the Telecom Industry and Consumers after the Introduction of Reliance Jio, *International Journal of Engineering and Management Research*, 9(3), 118-137.

66. Indumathy. R., Rajkumar, R. and Velmurugan.G., (2018) Jio's digital life – A survey, *International Journal of Recent Engineering Research and Development (IJRERD)*, 02(05), 71-74.

67. Jasrotia, S. S. Sharma, R. L. and Mishra, H. G. (2019) Disruptions in Indian Telecom Sector: A Qualitative Study on Reliance Jio, *IMJ*, 11(1), 37-45.

68. Joy, T. and Bahl, S. (2018) Disruption by Reliance Jio in Telecom Industry, *International Journal of Pure and Applied Mathematics*, 118(20), 43-4

69. Jyothika, M. J., (2019) Introduction of Reliance Jio and its Impact on telecom stocks at BSE", *IJARIIE*, 5(5), 658-666.

70. Kalyani, P. (2016) An Empirical Study on Reliance JIO Effect, Competitor's Reaction and Customer Perception on the JIO'S

Pre- Launch Offer, *Journal of Management Engineering and Information Technology (JMEIT)*, 3(5), 18-36 .

71. Lonare, A, Swamy, R and Srivastava, S, (2018) A Study on the Effect of Launch of Reliance Jio on Other Telecommunication Service Providers in India, *Pacific Business Review International*, 11(5), 111-122.

72. Laddha, S. and Trivedi, A., (2017) Customer perception towards brand Reliance Jio, *Asia Pacific Journal of Research in Business Management* 8(6). 1-17.

73. Mahalaxmi, K. R. and Kumar, S. N., (2017) Changing the Indian telecom sector: Reliance Jio, *International Journal of Advanced Research and Development*, 2(2), 62-64.

74. Medhi, M. (2017) A study on customer satisfaction level of using Reliance Jio network in Tezpur, Assam, *Journal of Marketing Strategy (JMS)* 5(3), 44-50.

75. Patlolla, R. and Doodipala, M. R. (2018) Distracting the Indian Telecommunications Sector: An Analytical Study on Reliance JIO Network, *American Journal of Marketing Research*, 4(2), 34-43

76. Santosh, R. and Rajandran, K. V. R (2018) A study on customer satisfaction on using Reliance-4G Jio service in Vallam-Thanjavur district, *International Journal of World Research*, I (LI), 40-44.

77. Salomi, S. and Selvan, K. G. (2017) Entry of Jio in Telecommunication Sector in A Competitive Environment, *International Journal of Research in Management & Business Studies* 4(3), 27-30.

78. Singh, R. (2017) Impact of Reliance JIO on Indian Telecom Industry: An Empirical Study, *International Journal of Scientific Research and Management (IJSRM)*, 5(07), 6469-6474.

79. Sisili, T. Kumar, S. Sivakumar, S. and Manikandan, G, (2018) A Study on Customer satisfaction towards Reliance Jio network, *IJIRT*, 4(12), 834-847.

80. Gautam, S., & Agarwal, A. (2022). The overall impact of Jio on the telecom industry of India - A study on BSNL. *International Journal of Mechanical Engineering, 7*(Special Issue), 608–613.

81. Editorial Staff. (2020, May 26). *Telecom industry in India, Jio impact and future.* The CEO Magazine India. Retrieved July 7, 2022, from https://www.theceo.in/blogs/telecom-industry-in-india-jio-impact-and-future

82. Bhalerao, V., & Deshmukh, A. (2019). Disruptive Innovation: Opportunities and Challenges. Sai Balaji International Journal of Management Sciences, 2(4), 41–47.

83. Juneja, P. (n.d.). *The Many Disruptions of the Indian Telecom Sector.* www.Managementstudyguide.Com. Retrieved June 7, 2022, from https://www.managementstudyguide.com/many-disruptions-of-indian-telecom-sector.htm

84. Sydle. (2022, March 10). *Disruptive Technologies You Need to Know.* Retrieved July 1, 2022, from https://www.sydle.com/blog/disruptive-technologies-61aa52868621853d1165bf07/

85. R. (2022, March 16). *Biggest Risks In Disruptive Innovation & Technology.* Resolver. Retrieved June 8, 2022, from https://www.resolver.com/blog/risks-disruptive-innovation-technology/

86. Rawat, A. (2020a, May 5). *Reliance Jio Covid-19 Data Breach In Focus On Lockdown Day 40.* Inc42 Media. Retrieved July 9, 2022, from https://inc42.com/buzz/startupsvscovid19-reliance-jio-covid-19-data-breach-comes-into-focus-on-lockdown-day-40/#:%7E:text=According%20to%20a%20report%20by,the%20performance%20of%20the%20website.

87. *Telecom industry witnesses' new trends amid disruptive technologies and an ever-rising demand from r.* (2021). India Brand Equity Foundation. Retrieved July 9, 2022, from https://www.ibef.org/research/newstrends/telecom-industry-witnesses-new-trends-amid-disruptive-technologies-and-an-ever-rising-demand-from-residences-and-enterprises

88. S. (2021, November 16). *Innovation Challenges.* MIT Enterprise Forum CEE. Retrieved July 9, 2022, from https://mitefcee.org/7-challenges-stopping-innovation-inyourorganization/#:%7E:text=%20What%20are%20 the%20challenges%20of%20innovation%3F%20,any%20 business%2C%20is%20determining%20who%20is. . .%20 More%20

89. *Disruptive Technology.* (2022, July 15). Drishti IAS. Retrieved July 20, 2022, from https://www.drishtiias.com/to-the-points/ paper3/disruptive-technology

90. Thapliyal, A. (2016, December 30). *5 problems that Reliance Jio needs to fix right away.* Business Today. Retrieved July 9, 2022, from https://www.businesstoday.in/technology/news/ story/5-problems-reliance-jio-69243-2016-12-30

91. *A literature review of disruptive innovation: What it is, how it works and where it goes - ScienceDirect.* (2020, April 8). A Literature Review of Disruptive Innovation: What It Is, How It Works and Where It Goes - ScienceDirect; www.sciencedirect. com. https://www.sciencedirect.com/science/article/abs/pii/ S0923474820300163

92. Juneja, P. (n.d.). *The Many Disruptions of the Indian Telecom Sector.* The Many Disruptions of the Indian Telecom Sector; www. managementstudyguide.com. Retrieved August 10, 2022, from https://www.managementstudyguide.com/many-disruptions-of- indian-telecom-sector.htm

93. Lakshminarayana N., Ramachandra K. (2019) Impact of Disruptive Innovation on Indian Telecom Sector - A Study. *International Journal of Trend in Scientific Research and Development (IJTSRD), 3(5),* 1615–1617. https://doi.org/ https://doi.org/10.31142/ijtsrd26687

94. Bakhit, W., (2016), *Impact of Disruptive Innovations on Mobile Telecom Industry in Lebanon*, International Journal of Research in Business and Social Science, 50(3), pp: 2147-2167.

95. GOVINDARAJAN, M. (2016, November 8). *Innovations in Telecom Industry*. One stop solution for GST, Income Tax, FEMA, SEZ, Import-Export and Corporate Laws in India, a useful portal for Professionals, trade and Industry. Retrieved August 14, 2022, from https://www.taxmanagementindia.com/visitor/detail_article.asp?ArticleID=7067

96. TRAI. (2018). *Evolution of Mobile Communications (1G, 2G and 3G)-Part I. April*, 1–6.

97. Tondare, S M, Panchal S D, Kushnure D T, Evolutionary steps from 1G to 4.5G, International Journal of Advanced Research in Computer and Communication Engineering, Vol. 3, Issue 4, April 2014.

98. Pankaj Sharma, Evolution of Mobile Wireless Communication Networks-1G to 5G as well as Future Prospective of Next Generation Communication Network, International Journal of Computer Science and Mobile Computing, Vol. 2, Issue. 8, August 2013, pg.47 – 53.

99. Roopali Sood, Atul Garg, Digital Society from 1G to 5G: A comparative study, International Journal of Application or Innovation in Engineering & Management (IJAIEM), Volume 3, Issue 2, February 2014.

100. HSPA - High Speed Packet Access, Retrieved from http://www.radio-electronics.com/info/cellulartelecomms/3g- hspa/umts-high-speed-packet-access-tutorial.php (Accessed on May 13, 2018).

101. LTE OFDM, OFDMA SC-FDMA & Modulation. Retrieved from http:// www. radio- electronics.com/info/cellulartelecomms/lte-long-term-evolution/lte-ofdm-ofdma-scfdma.php (Accessed on May 15, 2018).

102. K. Kumaravel, Comparative Study of 3G and 4G in Mobile Technology, 2nd Vol. 8, Issue 5, No 3, IJCSI International Journal of Computer Science Issues, pp. 256-263, September 2011.

103. Zeki Yetgin, Gamze Seckin, Progressive Download for 3G Wireless Multicasting International Journal of Hybrid Information Technology Vol. 1, No. 2, pp.67- 82, April2008.

104. Understanding 5G: Perspectives on Future Technological Advancements in Mobile, GSMA Intelligence, December 2014.

105. 3GPP TS 33.220 V15.0.0 (2017-06), 3rd Generation Partnership Project; Technical Specification Group Services and System Aspects; Generic Authentication Architecture (GAA); Generic Bootstrapping Architecture (GBA) (Release 15).

106. 3GPP TR 33.937 V14.0.0 (2017-03), 3rd Generation Partnership Project; Technical Specification Group Services and System Aspects; Study of Mechanisms for Protection against Unsolicited Communication for IMS (PUCI) (Release 14).

107. 5G Spectrum, Public Policy Position, November 2016, GSM Association.

108. TRAI. (2018). *Evolution of Mobile Communications (1G, 2G and 3G)-Part II May*, 1–8.

109. TondareS M, Panchal S D, Kushnure D T, Evolutionary steps from 1G to 4.5G, International Journal of

110. Advanced Research in Computer and Communication Engineering, Vol. 3, Issue 4, April 2014.

111. Panagiota D. Giotopoulou, The evolution of mobile communications: Moving from 1G to 5G, and from human-to-human to machine-to-machine communications, National and Kapodistrian University of Athens, School of Science, November 2015.

112. MN Bojouredi, Seidi Haghighat Shoar et al : Low Complexity Statistically Robust Precoder/Detector Computation for Massive

MIMO Systems, School of Electrical and Computer Engineering, University of Tehran, Tehran, Iran, 2017

113. Manar Mohaisen, YuPeng Wang, KyungHi Chang:The Graduate School of Information Technology and Telecommunications, INHA University, 2009

114. LTE OFDM, OFDMASC-FDMA & Modulation. Retrieved from http://www.radio-electronics.com/info/cellulartelecomms/lte-long-term-evolution/lte-ofdm-ofdma-scfdma.php (Accessed on May 15, 2018).

115. Understanding 5G: Perspectives on Future Technological Advancements in Mobile, GSMA Intelligence, December 2014.

116. 5G Spectrum, Public Policy Position, November 2016, GSM Association.

117. Emerging Trends in 5G/IMT2020, Geneva Mission Briefing Series, September 2016.

118. Understanding 5G: Perspectives on Future Technological Advancements in Mobile, GSMA Intelligence, December 2014.

119. The Evolution of Mobile technologies: 1G → 2G → 3G → 4G, Qualcomm, June 2014.

120. Jasrotia, S. S., Sharma, R. L., & Mishra, H. G. (2019). Disruptions in Indian Telecom Sector : A Qualitative Study on Reliance Jio. The Indore Management Journal, 11(1), 37–45.

121. Mahajan, V., Misra, R. and Mahajan, R. (2017) 'Review on factors affecting customer churn in telecom sector', *Int. J. Data Analysis Techniques and Strategies*, 9 (2), 122–144.

122. Srivastava, R., Bhangle, J., Bhatt, N., Gogri, K. and Marfatia, H. (2006). Role of competition in growing markets: Telecom sector. Indian journal of marketing, 36(9).

123. Kridel, D., Rappoport, P. and Taylor, L. (2002). The demand for high-speed access to the Internet. Forecasting the Internet. 11-22. Springer, Boston, MA.

124. Rappoport, P., Kridel, D.J., Taylor, L.D., Alleman, J. and Duffy-Deno, K.T. (2003). Residential demand for access to the Internet. Emerging telecommunications networks: The international handbook of telecommunications economics, 1, 55-72.

125. Mowen, J.C. (1980). On product endorser effectiveness: A balance model approach. Current issues and research in advertising, 3(1), 41-57.

126. Schultz, B. (2001). The m-commerce fallacy. Network World, 18(9), 77-77.

127. Sandhu, M.A., Mahasan, S.S., Rehman, A.U. and Muzaffar, S. (2013). Service Quality Dimensions Impact on Customer Satisfaction in Telecom Sector of Pakistan. Journal of Basic and Applied Scientific Research, 3(8), 27-34.

128. Malik, M.E., Ghafoor, M.M. and Hafiz, K.I. (2012). Impact of Brand Image, Service Quality and price on customer satisfaction in Pakistan Telecommunication sector. International journal of business and social science, 3(23).

129. Paulrajan, R. and Rajkumar, H., (2011). Service quality and customers preference of cellular mobile service providers. Journal of technology management & innovation, 6(1), 38-45.

130. Shastri, A. (2022). *Marketing Strategy of Reliance Jio - A 2022 Case Study*. IIDE. Retrieved July 2, 2022, from https://iide.co/case-studies/reliance-jio-marketing-strategy/

131. Scholar, D. (2022). Reliance Jio's Digital Marketing Strategies - Case Study. India's First Agency Styled Digital Marketing Training Institute. Retrieved August 2, 2022, from https://digitalscholar.in/reliance-jio-digital-marketing-strategies/

132. IndMoney. (2022). *Telecom Subscribers in India June 2022: Reliance Jio added another 4 million subscribers in June.* www.indmoney.com. Retrieved August 20, 2022, from https://www.indmoney.com/articles/stocks/telecom-subscribers-in-india-june-2022

133. Kashyap, H. (2022, August 18). June 2022 Telecom Data: Reliance Jio Adds 4.2 Mn Subscribers. Inc42 Media. Retrieved August 20, 2022, from https://inc42.com/buzz/reliance-jio-winning-streak-4-2-mn-subscribers-june-2022/

134. Telecom Regulatory Authority of India. (2022, June). Telecom Subscriptions Reports - TRAI (No. 53/2022). TRAI. https://www.trai.gov.in/sites/default/files/PR_No.53of2022_0.pdf

135. Staff, G. 3. (2017, September 5). Jio Turns One: 10 Ways the Indian Telecom Industry Changed After Jio Started Operations. Gadgets 360. Retrieved August 17, 2022, from https://gadgets360.com/telecom/features/jio-10-ways-the-indian-telecom-industry-changed-after-jio-started-operations-1746342

136. *Impact of Reliance's Entry.* (2018, February 20). Institute for Competitiveness. Retrieved August 18, 2022, from https://competitiveness.in/impact-of-reliance-entry/#:%7E:text=Highlights%20of%20the%20report%3A,accessibility%20and%20affordability%20of%20data.

137. Scholar, D. (2022, June 17). Reliance Jio's Digital Marketing Strategies - Case Study. India's First Agency Styled Digital Marketing Training Institute. Retrieved August 2, 2022, from https://digitalscholar.in/reliance-jio-digital-marketing-strategies/

138. Salomi, I. S., & Selvan, G. (2017). Entry of Jio in Telecommunication Sector in a Competitive Environment. International Journal of Research in Management & Business Studies, 4(3). www.ijrmbs.com

139. Abhinawa Talukdar and Monoj Kumar Chowdhury, The Novel Marketing Strategy of Reliance Jio that Forever Transfigured the Telecommunication Sector of India: A Study, International Journal of Management (IJM), 12(9), 2021, pp. 111-122. Retrieved from https://iaeme.com/Home/issue/IJM?Volume=12&Issue=9.